CAMBRIDGE STUDIES IN PHILOSOPHY

Realism and the progress of science

T0370852

CAMBRIDGE STUDIES IN PHILOSOPHY

General editor D. H. MELLOR

Advisory editors J. E. J. ALTHAM, SIMON BLACKBURN,
DANIEL DENNETT, MARTIN HOLLIS, FRANK JACKSON,
JONATHAN LEAR, T. J. SMILEY, BARRY STROUD

JAMES CARGILE *Paradoxes: a study in form and predication*
PAUL M. CHURCHLAND *Scientific realism and the plasticity of mind*
N. M. L. NATHAN *Evidence and assurance*
WILLIAM LYONS *Emotion*

Realism and the progress of science

Peter Smith

Cambridge University Press

CAMBRIDGE

LONDON   NEW YORK   NEW ROCHELLE
MELBOURNE   SYDNEY

CAMBRIDGE UNIVERSITY PRESS
Cambridge, New York, Melbourne, Madrid, Cape Town, Singapore, São Paulo, Delhi

Cambridge University Press
The Edinburgh Building, Cambridge CB2 8RU, UK

Published in the United States of America by Cambridge University Press, New York

www.cambridge.org
Information on this title: www.cambridge.org/9780521110341

© Cambridge University Press 1981

First published 1981
This digitally printed version 2009

A catalogue record for this publication is available from the British Library

Library of Congress Catalogue Card Number: 81–6151

ISBN 978-0-521-23937-0 hardback
ISBN 978-0-521-11034-1 paperback

Contents

Preface		vii
Introduction		1
1	A realist account of scientific progress	4
	1 The challenge of relativism	4
	2 Four questions for realism	10
2	The scrutability of reference	18
	1 Two doctrines of Quine's	18
	2 The inscrutability of reference of terms	21
	3 Identity and predication	27
	4 How to catch *gavagai*	33
3	A theory of interpretation	46
	1 The indeterminacy of translation of sentences	46
	2 Radical translation versus radical interpretation	51
	3 How determinate is interpretation?	58
4	Cluster theories of reference	70
	1 Natural kind predicates and proper names	70
	2 Kripke's remarks on naming	80
	3 A theory of reference for natural kind predicates	91
5	The account in perspective	104
	1 The story so far	104
	2 Atoms and molecules	106
	3 Phlogiston	112
	4 Mass	119
	Conclusion	125
	Bibliography	130
	Index	133

Preface

This book is concerned with the philosophical foundations of a realist explanation of the progress of science. I shall maintain that central to this explanation is the claim that there are many cases where competing or successive scientific theories are about the same things. I believe such a claim to be intuitively plausible. My principal aim, however, is not so much to champion this belief as to set down in a methodical way what the realist's explanation entails. As the reader will presently see, it raises some of the main problems in contemporary philosophy of language. In particular, the realist has to reply to several powerful *a priori* arguments directed against his position. Whether he can do so, and whether, therefore, he can fully substantiate his explanation of how science progresses, is, I believe, one of the most interesting questions in modern philosophy.

My approach in writing this book has been to try to give some background to the arguments I discuss rather than to assume the reader is fully conversant with them. One reason for this is that any one person's understanding of a complex argument tends to be different from any other person's. The result is that what appears to some to be germane criticism is regarded by others as beside the point. Another reason harks back to my own early years of studying philosophy. I recall finding it difficult sometimes to relate the abstruse argument of the moment to more mundane problems. What did it matter if we could not fully determine the intentions of speakers? Why should we have a theory of what it is for a name to refer? This puzzlement does not happen quite so often now, but for my fellow journeyers the occasional signpost or map reference seemed in order. I have thus tried to explain precisely how the resolution of a real and, I hope, fairly tangible problem – that of explaining the progress of science – depends on a host of complex arguments.

The basis of this book was a Ph.D. thesis submitted to the University of St. Andrews in 1978. During the intervening period it has seen substantial revision. I remain grateful, however, to St. Andrews for the assistance, financial and otherwise, which I earlier received. Perhaps like most authors I find it difficult in a preface to acknowledge fully the help and support of many teachers and friends. I hope that it is not invidious for me to take pleasure in mentioning in particular Leslie Stevenson and Nicholas Jardine; both gave most generously of their time. Between writing Chapter 5 of my thesis and the conclusion of this book, my wife Christine gave birth to two delightful children. In addition, she has even found time to encourage me and generally to make it possible for me to write. I shall always be thankful to her. As for Adam and Robert, they seem to concentrate more on making it *impossible* for me to write! But somehow they make me appreciate why I keep trying, and it is therefore to them that I dedicate this book.

P.J.S.   *Surrey*
                                                                        December 1980

Introduction

Philosophers of science have always been exercised by the problem of the extent to which scientific theories may be said to describe things that exist. We can characterize this problem as one of *reference*. It might be posed as a question: what can we say, on the basis of our scientific theories, about what there is in the world? The fundamental tenet of the realist's view of science is that those things referred to in a theory of an established science do exist. There are gravitational fields, muons and black holes, just as there are planets, mammals and bacteria. A second traditional problem has been that of whether it makes sense to describe scientific theories as true or false. This problem can be characterized as one of *predication*. Again the realist's answer is clear: the statements contained in a scientific theory are either true or false. For any given statement we may not now be in a position to say which it is, but we can at least conceive of what it would be for it to be true or false.

Though distinct, the problems of reference and predication are not divorced, for one way of explaining what it is for a statement to be true is by showing how things in the world can be as it says they are. According to such an account, what it means to say that the statement "Some bacteria require oxygen to survive" is true, is that there are such things as bacteria and oxygen and that some of the former require the latter if they are to survive. This form of relation between words and the world is often called a correspondence relation, and a theory of truth based on it a correspondence theory of truth. Although I shall not discuss this theory in detail in the book, the reader should note that it is often thought of as inseparable from, or even a corollary of, the realist's views on the problems of reference and predication.

Of much more interest to us is a third problem, closely related to those of reference and predication though perhaps of more recent concern: that of how we can explain the growth of science. By this is meant how we can explain what makes progress possible in science and how such progress comes about. For convenience we might describe this as the problem of *scientific progress*. On the basis of his answers to the problems of reference and predication, a realist is able to offer a plausible explanation. Theories of a science characteristically describe the behaviour of things that actually exist. Scientists, says the realist, act in accordance with this view, for they attempt to provide theories which better explain the behaviour of the same kinds of things already referred to by earlier theories. The progress of science is evidence that such a methodology works. In keeping with this the realist wants to say such things as that what Bohr identified as electrons earlier in this century, modern physicists do too; that most of the things Dalton classified as acids are similarly classified by our chemists; that temperature is nothing more than the measure of the mean kinetic energy of molecules; and that the planets Kepler recognized through Tycho Brahe's observations and to which he applied his laws of motion are just those to which Newton applied his laws of dynamics. The realist's central claim with respect to the problem of scientific progress is that there are many cases where competing or successive theories are about the same things.

The aim of this book is to defend such an account of the growth of science. In recent times it has been attacked from different quarters. Some philosophers of science have maintained that, far from the realist giving a plausible account of scientific progress, it does not even make sense to talk of a cumulative growth of true scientific belief. Such a relativist view has arisen from criticism of the explanations of scientific progress given by positivists and falsificationists. At the beginning of Chapter 1, I shall give a brief outline of this debate. Essentially the relativist holds that there is no one external reality which might be invoked to explain the truth or falsity of statements by members of linguistic communities more or less distant, in space or time, from our own. A correspondence theory of truth is denied. My objective will not be to assess the strength of this position. I shall regard it as a challenge to the realist to explain and defend his view of scientific progress. This I shall begin to do in the second section of the chapter where I pose four interconnected questions which a realist has to answer before his account of scientific progress is vindicated. These set the stage for the rest of the book.

Besides the considerations arising from the historiography of science, realism has been under attack in the philosophy of language.

2

The theory of reference is of central importance here. In fact, the complex of issues surrounding it constitute the core of this book, for I believe that the realist's account of scientific progress stands or falls with his account of what it is for a term to refer. The middle three chapters are therefore devoted to these matters. Chapter 2 deals with a general pragmatic argument which, if correct, would show that we cannot make sense of the notion of reference as classically conceived. Chapter 3 is concerned with another general argument which, in the present context, suggests that there are severe limitations to our understanding of previous scientific theories. If this argument were correct it would also cast doubt on any so-called "descriptive" theory of reference. This is important because, given my characterization of realism, a theory of reference is necessary for a realist account of scientific progress. In Chapter 4, I shall propose a descriptive theory of reference for scientific terms. It is here that my position directly challenges certain current orthodoxy in the philosophy of language, for descriptive theories of reference are generally thought of as non-realist or even anti-realist. I shall try to show that this need not be so.

In Chapter 5, the realist account which I shall defend is illustrated using three actual cases of theory change from the history of science. These add credence to the initial plausibility of the realist view. This is not to say, however, that every change of theory can be shown to reflect a cumulative growth in true scientific belief about what there is. Each case has to be looked at separately and in the end the truth of the realist view as a whole depends on certain contingent features associated with the interpretation of the theories of previous scientists.

Note. Throughout this book double quotation marks are used for shudder quotes and for mentioning terms while single quotation marks are used for quotations proper.

1

A realist account of scientific progress

1 THE CHALLENGE OF RELATIVISM

During this century, positivist and falsificationist explanations of
how scientific progress comes about have given rise to considerable
debate. According to the former there are two ways in which a
well-confirmed theory T, i.e., one which explains a large number of
observed regularities and has led to many successful predictions,
comes to be replaced. Firstly, we may extend T in order to predict
new phenomena. This, said the positivists, necessitates either the
introduction of new "correspondence rules" which define the
"theoretical terms" of T, or the supplementing of the theoretical
postulates and basic laws; in either case we obtain a closely related
new theory T'. We can then test T' against its predictions: if it proves
incorrect we reject it although we are free to retain T; if it proves
correct we accept T' and we are then free to press on to T'', etc. Once
we have established a theory like T we can work from it and so
increase our stock of scientific knowledge. An example of successful
theory extension is the development of the theory of mechanics.
Originally it was formulated to describe the motions of point-
masses, and was later extended to encompass the motions of rigid
bodies.

The second, and more complex, way in which the positivists
thought a well-confirmed theory comes to be replaced is when it is
reduced to, or subsumed under, a second theory which was originally formulated in a different area. Frequently cited examples
were the reduction of thermodynamics to statistical mechanics, the
subsumption of the laws of physical optics under quantum mechanics, and the reduction of Kepler's planetary laws and Galileo's terrestrial laws to Newtonian dynamics. Since the theories come from
different areas, the problem arises of relating their different terms.
"Heat", "temperature" and "entropy", for example, all occur in
thermodynamics whereas none of them occurs in statistical mechan-

ics. The positivists' approach to this problem was to require that, with the help of assumptions of some kind relating the "theoretical terms" of the theory being reduced to properties recognized by the theory to which it is being reduced, the laws of the former theory must be logically derivable from the body of the subsequent theory (Nagel 1961: 353 ff.). In terms of our example, thermodynamic laws concerning heat, temperature and entropy must, given certain assumptions, be logically derivable from the theory of statistical mechanics.

This idea of progress via theory reduction has been strongly criticized by Paul Feyerabend. His central claim is that the conditions laid down by the positivists are inapplicable to actual cases of theory change. One example he discusses in detail is the replacement of Galileo's terrestrial physics by Newtonian dynamics (Feyerabend 1962). If the positivists' condition of logical derivability is to be fulfilled, the laws of the former should be logically derivable from the latter. A basic assumption of Galileo's theory is that vertical accelerations in free fall near the earth's surface are constant over any finite (vertical) interval. Given Newton's theory, however, vertical accelerations in free fall are inversely proportional to distance from the earth. Admittedly, the difference may be experimentally indistinguishable, but that has no bearing on the fact that, strictly speaking, the two theories are logically inconsistent.

Feyerabend also challenges the condition, which he says is an immediate consequence of that of logical derivability, that the meanings of primitive descriptive terms remain the same through reduction. As a prime example he takes the reduction of classical mechanics to relativity theory. The classical theory assumes that the mass of a particle is constant and is conserved in all reactions in a closed system. According to relativity theory, however, the mass of a particle is proportional to its velocity relative to a co-ordinate system in which the observations are carried out. To appreciate that what is at issue here is a change in the meaning of the term "mass", one has to examine the structures of the theories and the roles played by the term in both. In the first place, different and (apparently) incompatible equations about mass hold in the two theories. Secondly, relativistic mass is a relation, involving relative velocities, between an object and a co-ordinate system, whereas classical mass is a property of the object itself and independent of its behaviour in co-ordinate systems. Nor will it do to identify the classical mass with

5

the relativistic rest mass, for although both may have the same numerical value, they cannot be represented by the same concept (Feyerabend 1965: 169).

Feyerabend's criticisms are not confined to the positivists' attempts to explain scientific progress; he also levels them at those of Sir Karl Popper and others who, for convenience, we might term falsificationists. Popper's conception of the nature of scientific theories and scientific progress was quite different from that of the positivists. According to him a theory or hypothesis is scientific if and only if it can be refuted or falsified by observational evidence. Theories are conjectures, or highly informative guesses about the world, and as such can be submitted to severe critical tests. In practice, however, it is never the case that a theory is rejected simply on the basis of its failing one or more empirical tests. For one theory to be rejected there has to be another which takes its place. The ideal situation is where we have two theories which both explain a large number of observed regularities but which predict different outcomes given the same experimental situation. In such cases we may appeal to 'crucial experiments' to decide between them. Some frequently cited examples of crucial experiments are: the behaviour of Mercury's perihelion, which was used as a crucial piece of evidence in favour of Einstein's theory and against Newton's; Young's two-slit experiment, which supported Huyghens' wave optics against Newton's semi-corpuscular theory; and Michelson and Morley's experiment which was used to discount the theory of the luminiferous ether in favour of the theory of relativity.

Another point of divergence between Popper and the positivists is that Popper rests no weight on the by now rather discredited claim that we can distinguish theoretical from observational scientific terms. For Popper, since any scientific term can support law-like statements, all scientific terms are to some extent theoretical. This naturally leads to an obvious and crucial question: a theory is refuted as a result of observations contrary to those it predicts, but if all terms are theoretical to some degree, what guarantee do we have that an observation report of a crucial experiment will enable us to decide between two *different* theories? Suppose we have two competing theories T^1 and T^2, and a crucial experiment E is proposed to decide between them. The terms used in reporting observations of E will have, according to Popper, some theoretical content; perhaps this content will be derived from T^1. But in that case why should we even suppose that it *could* support T^2 rather than T^1? We are on the brink of what Feyerabend foresees:

Each theory will possess its own experience, and there will be no overlap between these experiences. Clearly, a crucial experiment is now impossible. It is impossible not because the *experimental device* would be too complex or expensive, but because there is no universally accepted *statement* capable of expressing whatever emerges from observation. (1965: 214)

In outline, then, this is the substance of the attacks on positivist and falsificationist accounts of theory change. For our purposes the most important feature is the emphasis that Feyerabend places on the idea which constitutes perhaps the only thread common to both accounts: that in some way the meaning or import of a scientific term depends upon the theoretical context in which it occurs. The radical conclusion which appears to follow, and which Feyerabend hastens to draw, is that competing or successive theories may use the same terms but in principle there is no way of deciding whether or not they mean the same things by them. Such a situation has been described as one in which the theories concerned are incommensurable.

What bearing does this have on a realist's view of scientific progress? Fundamental to this view is the claim that competing or successive theories are often about the same things. Now Feyerabend defends the view that the ontology or domain of an earlier theory is completely replaced by that of a subsequent one. Strictly speaking, the only entities there are, are the ones contained in the ontologies of the theories we currently accept. To quote Feyerabend, 'introducing a new theory involves changes in the meanings of even the most "fundamental" terms of the language employed' (1962: 29). As a consequence of a rather different analysis of the history of science, Thomas Kuhn has reached a similar view with respect to theories separated by a 'scientific revolution'. An old scientific 'paradigm' is occasionally displaced by a new one, with the result that, in some senses at least, the post-revolutionary scientist finds himself working in a 'different world' (Kuhn 1970: Ch. 10). In short, for the relativist there is no one external reality by which we may measure the truth of our theories.

On the basis of a claim that the meanings of terms are different for different theories, the conclusion is drawn that what those terms refer to is different too. If this argument is valid it amounts to a flat contradiction of the realist's explanation of scientific progress. It is at

7

precisely this point, however, where a claim about meaning becomes a claim about reference, that we must look at recent work in the philosophy of language. In the first instance, at least, the realist's explanation seems only to rely on the concept of reference, for what he wants to show is that different theories are often about the same things, not that the terms they use have the same meaning. Consequently, if he can make good the distinction, it might be possible for him to concede that while we may not be able to decide whether terms mean the same intertheoretically it does not follow from this that we cannot decide whether they have the same reference.[1] This is a thesis which I shall refine in the coming chapters.

Before moving on it is to be noted that Feyerabend's position is not without its critics. It has been pointed out that in discussing the thesis of meaning variance, Feyerabend holds that apparently competing or rival theories may contain incompatible statements. But by maintaining that all the terms of such theories are incommensurable, i.e., that there is in principle no way of showing that they mean the same, it becomes obscure how certain of the statements contained in the theories could be shown to be incompatible (Shapere 1966). If there is no way of telling whether by 'mass' a Newtonian means the same as an Einsteinian, then when the former assents to the sentence "Mass is a constant property of an object" and the latter dissents from it there is no way of telling whether they are even assenting to and dissenting from the same statement; they are talking past each other. Showing that statements from different theories are incompatible appears to involve at least the possibility of *translating* from one to the other. The possibility of translation, however, is precisely what incommensurability denies.

What must be recognized, however, is that criticism of one position does not in itself establish the earlier view which was being brought into question. Scepticism about Feyerabend's relativist claims regarding theory change does not in itself tell in favour of positivism, falsificationism or, more importantly for our purpose, realism. In defence of his claim of sameness of reference, the realist has first to make good the distinction between meaning and reference.

As a result of the work of Frege, such a distinction has been the

---

[1] An early version of this view was advanced by Israel Scheffler (1967: Ch. 3). It should be noted that although I shall maintain that a theory of reference is a necessary condition for making sense of scientific progress, there are some realists, notably Wilfrid Sellars (1968: 81ff.; 1973), who have pursued a different line.

subject of extensive discussion in recent philosophy of language. In his 1892 paper 'Über Sinn und Bedeutung', he distinguishes the 'Sinn' or "sense" of a proper name from its 'Bedeutung' or "reference". Reference signifies the relation between a word and an object. It is that which we use the name to talk about and so forms no part of what we might ordinarily think of as meaning. Sense is more closely related to meaning. Knowing the sense of a name – understanding it – enables one in principle to decide which object, if any, the name refers to; but there being a relation in the first place is something different. Frege does not actually talk about sense being part of a more general notion. Nevertheless, it is clear that within the intuitive notion of meaning he thought that a distinction could be drawn between sense and two other ingredients: "force", as in the difference between asserting something and asking whether it is true, and "tone", as in the difference between "sweat" and "perspiration". These last two ingredients, however, will not concern us in this book. We shall be concentrating on sentences in the indicative mood and our analysis will scarcely touch the subtleties of tone.

Before suggesting how we might extend Frege's original insight, let me say a few words about terminology. Many scientific terms are predicates, i.e., expressions of the form ". . . is a ψ" or ". . . is φ", where the blank is to be filled by a singular term such as a name or a definite description to yield a complete sentence. In talking of a singular term I shall sometimes say that it *denotes* an object, by which I mean that it refers to the object, and sometimes that such an object is the *referent* of the term. In the case of a predicate I shall simply talk of its *extension*, by which I mean the set of objects to which it can be correctly applied. The notion of reference is to be understood broadly as signifying not only the relation between a singular term and an object but also the relation between a predicate and a set of objects. So when I talk about a theory of reference for scientific terms this is sometimes to be understood as meaning a theory of the extensions of scientific predicates.

Returning to the problem of theory comparability, suppose that theory T^1 has the following empirical consequence:

(i) $(x) (Px \supset Qx)$

Suppose also that an apparent rival, T^2, has the empirical consequence:

(ii) $(\exists x) (Px \, \& \sim Qx)$

Ordinarily we should maintain that, since (i) and (ii) are logical contradictories, T^1 and T^2 are in conflict. In maintaining this we are committed to holding not that both P and Q have the same *sense* in both T^1 and T^2 but that they have the same *extension*. The reason is that, in extensional logic, to say that (i) and (ii) are contradictories is to say that they could not both be true under any uniform interpretation of the predicates, where by 'uniform interpretation of the predicates' is meant: given a non-empty domain of objects D, and an interpretation I which assigns sets of objects to predicates as their extensions, all occurrences of the same predicate letter under an interpretation I are construed as having the same extension. If it can be established that both P and Q have the same extension as they occur in T^1 and T^2, then they can be represented, as in (i) and (ii), by the same predicate letter in logical form. Finally, no uniform interpretation of the predicates could make both (i) and (ii) true. In order to justify his claim that competing or successive theories can be about the same things, then, the realist's main task is to establish what the extensions of predicates from the theories are and to express this in such a way as to permit comparison.

2 FOUR QUESTIONS FOR REALISM

Let me spell out in more detail the realist account of scientific progress which I shall defend in this book. To begin with we need to be more definite about what sort of predicates are to have their extensions compared. If we look at some typical problematic cases of theory change, we come across questions like "Are the formative elements postulated by Mendel the genes studied by modern molecular biologists?", "Were the atomic theories of Dalton and Avogadro about the same things?", and "When Newton used the term 'gravitational field', did it apply to anything recognized in relativity physics?". Less problematic cases, i.e., ones where sameness of extension is more obvious, are Ptolemaic and Copernican theories of the planets, Aristotle's theory of the brain and that of contemporary neurophysiologists, and even the discovery that whales are mammals and not fish. In all of these cases, the relevant predicate – "gene", "atom", "gravitational field", "planet", "brain", and "whale" – is a *natural kind predicate*. Such predicates, which can be correctly applied to objects on the basis of their physical properties, occupy a central place in scientific theorizing. At the beginning of Chapter 4, I shall talk about them in more detail. I shall also mention examples of theory change, to be discussed in the final chapter, which involve predicates not associated with natural kinds. For the present, however, I wish to restrict my investigations to the central cases of natural kind predicates.

The most general question for a realist account of the growth of scientific knowledge, then, is:

(1) How can we compare the extensions of relevant natural kind predicates from different scientific theories?

Although this question is intended in a material sense, as a question about the means that are to be employed in actually ascertaining what the relevant predicates of different theories have as their extensions in such a way as to permit comparison, it can also be understood more formally. In the formal sense it is a question about the logic of theory comparison: what language or theory should we use for comparing the extensions of natural kind predicates from two distinct theories? Let me digress briefly to answer this question.

Suppose a realist is considering two apparently rival or successive theories T^1 and T^2. He wants to establish that the key predicate P of T^1 has the same extension as the key predicate Q of T^2. To begin with he should not be construed as trying to establish the truth of the proposition "$(x)\ (Px \equiv Qx)$", for this very proposition, in virtue of the range of both P and Q being bound by the same quantifier, assumes that T^1 and T^2 are comparable. He needs to take a more circumspect approach, and the way to do this is to *mention*, or talk about the extension of, the predicates P and Q rather than to *use* them. That is, he aims to assert both "The extension of P is . . ." and "The extension of Q is . . ." in the same language. Since Tarski (1956), a language in which one can in this way talk about the terms of another is commonly referred to as a *metalanguage*. A metalanguage provides a way of saying what the extension of a predicate of an object language is, and thereby provides a means of comparing different predicates.

Having outlined how question (1) should be dealt with when understood in a formal sense, let me now return to its material sense. In concentrating on reference, a realist has to be able to meet the challenge, arising from the claim that different theories are incommensurable, that there is no way of deciding whether or not predicates from different scientific theories have the same extensions. He therefore has to give a general account of how the extensions of

11

relevant predicates can be discovered, i.e., an account of how we are to decide which things a particular predicate can be, or was, correctly applied to.

In pursuing an investigation into the epistemological question of how we decide what a particular scientific predicate has, or had, as its extension, a realist will sometimes be led to consider terms, such as "whale", "planet" and "brain" to continue the above examples, which have a use outside science. Many natural kind predicates are like this. Often this feature will be of some help in understanding what the extensions of terms used in past scientific theories were. The more widely a term is used within a linguistic community, the more information will be available to one who wishes to understand what it means and what it refers to. A study of the use of a natural kind predicate, then, is best construed as a study of its use not just within a particular scientific theory, but within a linguistic community. I shall discuss these points more fully in subsequent chapters. For the present, we are now in a position to formulate the second of the four questions facing the realist's account of scientific progress:

(2) How can we discover which objects belong to the extension of a natural kind predicate as that predicate is used within a linguistic community?

It is my contention that the most obvious way to answer question (1) is by answering question (2). Now it might be suggested that there is in fact a stronger relation between the two, namely that an answer to the second is a necessary condition for an answer to the first. How can we, it might be said, *compare* the extensions of two predicates from different theories without first being able to discover *what* their extensions are? I have much sympathy with this position, but it is not one which I shall, or need to, defend. The contrary position is that the notion of reference can only be constructed by abstracting from that of co-reference and that therefore the first question is prior to the second. We can only make sense, so this argument would run, of the notion of any one predicate having an extension in so far as we appreciate what it is for two predicates to have the same extension. On the face of it this position seems counter-intuitive, but I shall not press the point here, for my aim is simply to firmly ground *a* realist view of the progress of science. In order to meet the challenge posed by the thesis of incommensurability, both questions (1) and (2) have to be answered. My approach will be to answer (2) before (1).

What sorts of considerations will have to be taken into account when it comes to answering (2)? I have discussed the Fregean distinction between the sense of a term and its reference or extension, and noted that associated with the sense is a criterion for determining the reference or extension. I also said that sense could be considered as the primary notion constitutive of meaning. Thus we might expect that the sense of a scientific predicate will be given, at least in part, by the theoretical principles used in stating the theory, or theories, in which it occurs. But the realist has to be extremely careful here. Suppose for the moment that the realist wishes to construe the statement that the sense of a scientific predicate is given in part by theoretical principles as saying that there is, associated with the sense, a criterion, satisfaction of which is a *necessary* condition for an object's belonging to the extension. Then in nearly every case of theory change he will *not* be able to show that successive theories are about the same things! Putnam has offered a vivid example:

Bohr assumed in 1911 that there are (at every time) numbers p and q such that the (one dimensional) position of a particle is q and the (one dimensional) momentum is p; if this was part of the meaning of 'particle' for Bohr, and in addition, 'part of the meaning' means 'necessary condition for membership in the extension of the term', then electrons are *not* particles in Bohr's sense, and, indeed, there are *no* particles 'in Bohr's sense'. (And no 'electrons' in Bohr's sense of 'electron', etc.) None of the terms in Bohr's 1911 theory referred! It follows on this account that we cannot say that present electron theory is a better theory of the same particles that Bohr was referring to. (1973: 197)

From this the realist does not conclude that the terms of Bohr's theory were like, for example, the term "phlogiston", which we now say cannot be correctly applied to anything at all. He prefers to say that some of Bohr's beliefs about electrons, etc., and hence some of his theoretical postulates about them, were mistaken. Similar remarks might be made concerning, say, Ptolemy's beliefs about the planets – he thought they orbited the earth – and Muller's beliefs about genes – he thought they were composed of proteins. But to maintain this, while holding that modern researchers are talking about the same things, means that satisfying the full sense of a term cannot be thought necessary for an object's being a member of that term's extension, or, in the case of a singular term, for its being referred to by that term.

Two points follow from this. The first is that we shall not be concerned with what Muller, Bohr, Ptolemy, etc., "had in mind" or "intended to refer to" when they used terms like "gene", "electron" and "planet". What they had in mind may be revealed by more general considerations to do with what they said, how they acted, and what they believed. Our concern, on the other hand, is with what they *succeeded* in referring to, where success is judged relative to our present understanding. The most striking results of this arise in theories claiming to be about caloric, phlogiston, magnetic flux, and the luminiferous ether, where we now say that those terms fail to refer or have an extension.

The second point is that it is incumbent upon the realist, in so far as he wants to continue to use the notion of "sense", to reject the view that there is always a single core of descriptions associated with a term, satisfaction of which is a necessary and sufficient condition for an object's being a member of that term's extension, or for its being denoted by that term. The realist has to allow for error, for mistaken belief, not only on the part of our predecessors but also on the part of ourselves. Putnam has attempted to avoid this difficulty by abandoning the notion of "sense" altogether and using what has come to be known as a *causal* account of reference (1973; 1975a). In Chapter 4, I shall criticize this strategy and offer an alternative based on a *cluster* theory of reference.

The causal account emphasizes features of our use of proper names and natural kind predicates which are relevant to answering the *epistemological* question of how we can discover what a term refers to or has as its extension. If we can discover certain facts about the causal origin of a theory – what apparatus and data a scientist or group of scientists had available before advancing a theory – this might enable us to rule out some conjectures as to a predicate's extension, or enable us to settle more quickly on others. In this way the causal account, so I shall argue, is relevant to answering question (2). What it is not relevant to is answering the *conceptual* question of what it is for a proper name to refer or for a predicate to have an extension. Moreover, it seems clear that this latter question should be answered first: we have to know what it is for a predicate to have an extension before we can decide what the extension of a particular predicate is. Hence we have a third question for realism:

(3) What conditions have to be satisfied by a natural kind predi-
     cate "φ" and an object a in order for "φ", as it is used within a
     linguistic community C, to be correctly applied to a?

As with the relation between questions (1) and (2), it should be noted that I am only maintaining that the most obvious way of answering question (2) is by answering question (3), not that an answer to (3) is a necessary condition for an answer to (2). If one did hold that the notion of reference can be constructed only by abstracting from that of co-reference, i.e., if one held that an answer to question (2) depended on there being an answer to question (1), then apparently an answer to question (2) would not depend on there being an answer to question (3). Perhaps question (3) would be rejected as unanswerable. Indeed, this might be the very reason for inverting what I called the most obvious relation between (1) and (2). But it is not an alternative which I shall discuss, for I believe that question (3) can be answered. I shall, however, continue to make a clear distinction between questions (2) and (3). (2) is an epistemological question, (3) a question of conceptual analysis. By way of analogy, consider the two questions "How can we discover who the father of a given person is?" and "What is it to be a father?". The former is epistemological, the latter conceptual. There are various tests and criteria for discovering paternity, but obviously their very existence presupposes to a certain extent that it is understood what it is to be a father.

Although there is an important distinction here, we might expect that once we have formulated an answer to the conceptual question this will suggest criteria for answering the epistemological one. An explanation of what it is to be a father clarifies the relation of paternity and so enables us to devise criteria for discovering who a person's father is. In Chapter 4, I shall argue that a predicate "φ" can be correctly applied to an object if and only if that object satisfies a suitable majority of those descriptions believed to be true of φs. This suggests that, in order to discover what a particular natural kind predicate has as its extension, we shall have to determine what is or was believed, by users of the predicate, to be true of things of that kind. But this is not to say that "belief" is, as it were, the only category with which the realist has to work. For it is at this stage, i.e., the stage of answering a particular instance of (2), that he can make good use of the causal account of reference. In Chapter 3, I shall also suggest other criteria that might aid him in discovering the extensions of scientific predicates.

Questions of sameness or difference of extension relate primarily to understanding previous scientific theories. The problems of understanding the language associated with a theory will also be compounded in these cases. The realist might even be forced to recognize that, despite the constraints alluded to above, he cannot always determinately *translate* from another language to his own. He would then have to decide if such indeterminacy affects the question of what reference or extension a term has, or whether it merely affects the sense. I shall have a lot more to say about these issues later, but first we need to pose a final question.

So far in this book I have assumed that there is a relation of reference between language and the world. That there is such a relation might seem obvious; certainly we have seen no cause to doubt its existence so far. If there were not then the realist's position, as I understand it and have outlined it, would not even get off the ground. The realist represents the scientist as one who postulates theories describing the real world. Moreover, the scientist is not usually thought to be privileged in thus making contact with "external reality"; most of us, most of the time, think, act and talk as though we do. But how determinate is the relation between language and the world? In the next chapter, I shall consider a forceful argument presented by Quine for the view that even though there is some relation between language and the world it is not that which philosophers since Frege have called reference. I shall then be dealing with a fourth question for realism:

(4) Is there a determinate relation of reference between natural kind predicates, as used within linguistic communities, and sets of objects?

An explanation of what it is for a singular term to denote or for a predicate to have an extension, of how we can discover which objects a given predicate can be correctly applied to, and hence whether or not predicates from different scientific theories have the same extensions all depends on there being a primitive or fundamental relation of reference between language and the world.

Having posed these four questions and explained how the most obvious way to answer each one is by first answering any and all of those following it, the way forward should be clear. With reference to the most basic question, (4), I shall consider, in Chapters 2 and 3, two important doctrines of Quine's: the inscrutability of reference of terms and the indeterminacy of translation of sentences. Once I have clarified the relation between these, I shall aim to establish, in Chapter 2, that Quine has not succeeded in showing that reference is inscrutable, either in our own home language or when it comes to translating an alien language. On the basis of this I shall answer question (4) in the affirmative. Before going on to present, in Chapter 4, an answer to question (3) based on a cluster theory of reference for natural kind predicates, I shall devote Chapter 3 to building up a theory of interpretation which takes into account Quine's arguments for indeterminacy of translation. This will *inter alia* suggest the threads of an answer that can later be used for question (2). One of my main contentions in supporting a cluster theory will be that it is grounded in, and indeed makes essential use of, a theory of interpretation. I shall also base several of my arguments for a cluster theory with respect to natural kind predicates on what I shall claim are analogous arguments with respect to proper names. At the beginning of Chapter 5, I shall explain how question (2) is to be answered. I shall then go on to answer question (1) in relation to three particular historical cases.

2

The scrutability of reference

Twenty years have passed since Quine's *Word and Object* was first published. In the now famous Chapter II, 'Translation and Meaning', it is argued that a certain systematic indeterminacy attaches to the enterprise of translation. As Quine (1970) has subsequently emphasized, however, there are two main strands of argument for this conclusion which need to be distinguished. The first, which constitutes 'the real ground' of the doctrine of the indeterminacy of translation of sentences, turns on the underdetermination of physical theory by all possible evidence. To use Quine's own metaphor, underdetermination maximizes the scope of the doctrine by 'pressing from above' (1970: 183). The second is that which he calls 'the inscrutability of reference of terms', and this is the strand which I shall be concentrating on in this chapter.

Despite his subsequent clarification, the relation of indeterminacy of translation to inscrutability of reference is not straightforward. On the one hand, inscrutability extends the scope of indeterminacy by 'pressing from below' (Quine 1970: 183); on the other, 'the inscrutability of terms need not always bring indeterminacy of sentence translation in its train' (1970: 182). Apparently, then, inscrutability does not imply indeterminacy. For convenience, let us express this by:

(i) Ins $\nrightarrow$ Ind

Let us now assume, for the sake of simplicity, that inscrutability can be treated as the negation of scrutability, and indeterminacy as the negation of determinacy. They might in fact be thought of as stronger notions, perhaps containing modal expressions, but they are presumably at least this. We may then rephrase (i) as:

(ii) $\sim$Scr $\nrightarrow$ $\sim$Det

From (ii) it follows that determinacy of sentence translation does not imply scrutability of reference of terms, i.e., we might be able determinately to translate some foreign sentence without being able to scrutinize the reference of its terms. Hence:

(iii) Det $\nrightarrow$ Scr

This makes sense of what Quine says (1970) about his examples of the Japanese classifiers and deferred ostension.

The general issue that I want to investigate in this chapter is whether Quine's doctrines of indeterminacy of translation and inscrutability of reference suggest that there is not a determinate relation of reference between natural kind predicates (as used within linguistic communities) and sets of objects. Clearly the doctrine of inscrutability is particularly relevant since it seems to be aimed at precisely the claim that there is such a determinate relation. Whether or not the doctrine of *indeterminacy* is relevant would seem to depend on whether scrutability of reference of terms implies determinacy of translation of sentences, i.e., on whether:

(iv) Scr $\rightarrow$ Det

is true. If it is then, by similar reasoning to the above, we may conclude that:

(v) Ind $\rightarrow$ Ins

is true. Consequently there would be further reason for doubting the claim that there is a determinate relation of reference. Unfortunately, Quine has been reticent with respect to (v), though it would seem to be a thesis which he might readily accept. Nevertheless, there do seem to be good reasons for thinking (iv), and therefore (v), false. As I progress with my discussion of the indeterminacy doctrine in the next chapter, I shall suggest what some of them are. I shall thus maintain that, if it can be shown that Quine's doctrine of the *inscrutability* of reference of terms is not well founded, he has failed to demonstrate that there is not a determinate relation of reference between natural kind predicates and sets of objects. This will in turn be considered sufficient for the conclusion that there is a certain primitive relation of reference between language and the world, the one which we have seen the realist maintain to hold between natural kind predicates and sets of objects. The most fundamental question in the realist's account of the growth of science will thus be answered in the affirmative.

When discussing question (1) of the previous chapter in a formal sense, I said that we use a metalanguage in order to specify the relations between predicates of an object language and their extensions. The same goes for specifying the relations between singular terms of an object language and their referents. The metalanguage enables us to mention the expressions of the object language. Those cases in which we are particularly interested are where the object language contains a scientific theory, i.e., all of the terms used in stating the theory are assumed to belong to the language. When we wish to talk about the terms of the theory, any metalanguage constructed over the object language in the Tarskian manner will suffice. Often, however, we wish to know what relations hold between expressions of one theory and those of another; relations such as co-referentiality and coextensiveness. This other theory might be a more comprehensive theory in the sense that its domain includes that of the first. On the other hand, it might just be another theory related more loosely; the domains overlap. Another alternative still would be that there is no overlap whatsoever, in which case the theories have different domains. In order to permit comparison, however, we must in all cases be able to talk about the terms of both theories using the *same* metalanguage. Otherwise we shall be unable to say anything at all about the relations that interest us, not even, for example, that the extensions of certain predicates are different.

This central idea, that we must use a background language for talking about connections between words of an object language and the objects in the world, suggests to Quine that the only relations which really make sense are those between one language and another, not those between language and the world. Perhaps the key points in his argument for this view are that, from the standpoint of a different background language, the connections might be different, and that we have no telling reason for preferring one background language to another. Using a favourite example, Quine puts the first point like this:

When we ask, 'Does "rabbit" really refer to rabbits?' someone can counter with the question: 'Refer to rabbits in what sense of "rabbits"?' thus launching a regress; we need the background language to regress into. The background language gives the query sense, if only relative sense; sense relative in turn to it, this background language. (1969a: 49)

This idea of 'ontological relativity' he conjoins with the second point to draw the conclusion that 'what makes sense is to say not what the objects of a theory are, absolutely speaking, but how one theory of objects is interpretable or reinterpretable in another' (1969a: 50).

Hartry Field has argued that this conclusion seems to rule out even the possibility of a correspondence theory of truth (1974). As I noted in the Introduction, this kind of theory attempts to explain the notion of truth by appealing to a correspondence relation between words of a language and objects in the world. I also noted that it is sometimes thought of as a corollary to a realist view of the problems of reference and predication. As Field sees it, Quine's conclusion only permits correspondence between the words of one theory and the words of another, not between words and objects. In responding, Field argues that *even if* Quine is right about the inscrutability of reference, and in fact Field does not think he is (1974: 202–3), we ought still to accept a correspondence theory of truth and reject the conclusion that the only relation which makes sense is that between the words of one theory and the words of another. As there is nothing in this which conflicts with the realist position I am advocating, I shall not discuss it further. What will be of concern to us later, in Chapter 4, is that Field also argues that his position is only possible if we base our semantic theory on 'various *generalizations* of the notions of denotation and signification – for example, the notions of partial denotation and partial signification' (1974: 209). For the present, however, let us return to Quine's claim that there is no fact of the matter about reference. This might be seen as a radical form of the incommensurability thesis, for it questions whether there is any determinate relation between language and the world. Quine's argument is therefore directed at the very foundations of realism. Let us look at it in detail.

2 THE INSCRUTABILITY OF REFERENCE OF TERMS

To begin with, Quine argues for the inscrutability of reference in the translation of predicates, or, as he usually calls them, general terms, from a foreign language for which we have no previously established dictionary. Thus, to take Quine's notorious example, suppose that a field linguist is wondering how to translate the foreign term *"gavagai"* into English. He is able to establish inductively, beyond reasonable doubt, that a foreigner can be prompted to assent to the occasion sentence "*Gavagai*" by the presence of a rabbit, or reasonable facsimile, and not otherwise. The obvious translation for the term would seem to be "rabbit". But, Quine notes, 'a whole rabbit is present when and only when an undetached part of a rabbit is present; also when and only when a temporal stage of a rabbit is present'.[1] There is no way of telling, simply by ostension, which of "rabbit", "undetached rabbit part" or "rabbit stage" is the correct translation. Using Quine's terminology, "*Gavagai*" in the foreign tongue can be established as having the same 'stimulus meaning' as, i.e., as being 'stimulus synonymous' with, the English "Rabbit". This means, roughly, that each occasion sentence would be assented to, or dissented from, by a speaker of the relevant language if asked under the same conditions of sensory stimulation. "Rabbit", however, is in turn stimulus synonymous with the other English occasion sentences "Undetached rabbit part" and "Rabbit stage". As Quine sees it, trying to settle behaviourally the extensions of the various terms constituting these behaviourally indistinguishable sentences is an insoluble, and therefore unreal, problem. Though it is obvious that the extensions of the various English terms must be distinct, there seems no aspect of actual or possible physical behaviour which tells us to which of them the linguist should map "*gavagai*".

How is the linguist to decide between the alternatives? Well, says Quine, he has to turn from ostension and observed behaviour to verbal stimuli and verbal behaviour. In English, our recognition of sortal terms – terms which divide their extensions – depends on grammatical particles and constructions like plural endings, pronouns, numerals, the "is" of identity, and its related terms "some" and "other". The linguist proceeds by abstracting what he takes to be similar particles and constructions from the foreign language and hypothesizing how they are to be associated with the English ones. Such hypotheses of translation Quine calls 'analytical hypotheses' (1960: Section 15).

The linguist may now ask the foreigners what he supposes amounts to the questions "Same *gavagai*?" or "How many *gavagais*?". Their answers would seem to settle matters. Quine agrees that to select a foreign word, say "*bleg*", as the identity particle

---

[1] 1969a: 30. In 1960: section 12, 'the rabbit fusion' and 'manifestation of rabbithood' are added as further alternatives. These will be considered towards the end of Section 4 of this chapter.

virtually fixes the translation; hence some analytical hypotheses are of crucial importance. But they are after all only hypotheses, themselves underdetermined by behaviour. Imagine that a foreigner sees, protruding from behind a small rock, a rabbit head and a tail. He is prompted to utter the sentence: *"Ip gavagai bleg op gavagai"*. The linguist might equally well translate it as "This rabbit is the same as that one" or as "This undetached rabbit part belongs with that one".

The possibility thus emerges that there are incompatible manuals of translation for predicates from a foreign language to our home language which would preserve invariant all the dispositions to physical and verbal behaviour on the part of speakers of the foreign language. The manuals are incompatible in the sense that they would carry a single predicate from the foreign language into various predicates of the home language which are not coextensional. So failure of reference, not merely failure of sense – which I shall later argue to be the import for sentence translation of the underdetermination of physical theory by evidence – is what is at issue.

Two features of this argument require further comment. The first is that Quine pays exclusive attention to the behavioural facts – ostension, verbal behaviour and the like – when considering how the linguist might fix on a particular translation manual. The study of language and the meanings it contains is, for Quine, primarily a study of behaviour, 'language is a social art which we all acquire on the evidence solely of other people's overt behaviour under publicly recognizable circumstances' (1969a: 26). Viewed correctly then, 'knowledge, mind, and meaning are part of the same world that they have to do with, and . . . are to be studied in the same empirical spirit that animates natural science. There is no place for a prior philosophy' (ibid.). Consequently there is nothing more to guide us in translating the language of another person than that person's dispositions to overt behaviour.

The second feature is that Quine thinks it is obvious that there are no behavioural facts underlying the use of a term like *"gavagai"* which could allow us to say that it is a predicate signifying one set under translation rather than another. That is, no behavioural facts give us a reason for preferring one translation to another. As we saw, appeal to the foreigner's dispositions to assent and dissent to verbal stimuli fails to resolve the indeterminacy, since we then have to allow for the indeterminacy of translation of identity and other individuative apparatus. For someone now to say that there is some fact of the matter as regards the translation, even though it cannot be decided by appeal to behavioural facts, is for him to fall victim to what Quine derides as 'the myth of a museum in which the exhibits are meanings and the words are labels' (1969a: 27).

Having noted these two features of the argument, let us see how Quine develops it. In place of the foreigner and translation from a remote language, let us put a neighbour of ours and our own home language. We become linguists ourselves, wondering how to "translate" our neighbour's English discourse. Ordinarily we are guided by one compendious, analytical hypothesis, viz., the rule of homophonic translation: we equate expressions in our neighbour's mouth with the same strings of phonemes in our own. Sometimes there is a 'principle of charity' at work whereby we avoid attributing absurdity to our neighbour in certain untoward situations, but by and large homophony suffices. Yet there is nothing in either the neighbour's behaviour, or dispositions to behave, which obliges us to adopt this rule. There are no behavioural facts, so the argument goes, to prevent us adopting heterophonic translations whereby his "is the same as" carries over into our "belongs with" and his "rabbit" into our "undetached rabbit part", and so on across the language:

> We can reconcile all this with our neighbour's verbal behaviour, by cunningly readjusting our translations of his various connecting predicates so as to compensate for the switch of ontology. In short, we can reproduce the inscrutability of reference at home. (1969a: 47)

The final stage of the argument comes when we wonder about our own discourse and our own dispositions. The same points that were made concerning our interpretation of our neighbour's speech may be made *mutatis mutandis* when it comes to interpreting our own. As Quine says, 'if there is really no fact of the matter, then the inscrutability of reference can be brought even closer to home than the neighbour's case; we can apply it to ourselves' (ibid.).

The upshot is that there will be non-identical mappings onto itself of the infinite set of sentences of some one speaker's language which preserve invariant all his dispositions to assent to or dissent from sentences. As was the case in translating from a foreign language, those sentences onto which some one sentence is mapped will be different, though stimulus synonymous, because a single predicate will be mapped onto predicates that are (intuitively) not coextensive. What is different, however, is that all of the predicates involved will be predicates of the *same* language. The theory of reference is at issue here, not just the theory of translation.

This development by Quine of his argument from translation challenges the very foundations of the realist position as I have explained it. If there is no determinate relation of reference between expressions of a language and parts of the world, it becomes difficult to see how questions (1) – (3) posed in the previous chapter could possibly be answered. In consequence, one might be led to speculate on how much is left of realism when based on a weaker words/world relation such as might be distilled from Quine's notion of stimulus meaning. Such speculation, however, must surely signal a departure from the Fregean tradition. We can only make sense of saying what the objects of a theory are relative to some background language. But, if Quine is right, there are no behavioural facts which justify the preference of one assignment within a background language to others, and hence no fact of the matter as to which assignment is correct.

As Quine himself has observed, the example of rabbits and their parts and stages is both contrived and perverse. He goes on to present less bizarre cases that arise in practice. The clearest involves a claim about incompatible but equally acceptable translations of certain Japanese classifiers (1969a: 35–8). Moving to the home language, others are said to arise when we use deferred ostension to establish some correspondence, as in the case of a petrol gauge. This suggests there might be an inscrutability in the choice between expressions and, say, their Gödel numbers as referents for quoted expressions. Finally, Quine has elsewhere expressed a guarded acceptance of Harman's example of the various referents of numerical expressions given by competing set theoretic reductions of number (1970: 183).

Nevertheless, perversity is often the order of the day when it comes to philosophical disputation. What is so important about the *gavagai* example and its development to include terms of our own language is that it opens up the possibility that *every* predicate that divides its reference does so inscrutably. The Japanese classifiers example involves inscrutability only in translation. As for the indecision about expressions and their Gödel numbers (also said by Quine to be a perverse example), the ground is precisely the same as for inscrutability at home; we need to be able to readjust our translations of connecting predicates. One comes to realize that the vital step in each of these examples is the one summed up by Quine in this passage:

The whole notion of terms and their denotation is bound up with our own grammatical analysis of the sentences of our own language. It can be projected on the native language only as we settle what to count in the native language as analogues of our pronouns, identity, plurals, and related apparatus. (1970: 181–2)

Quine finds this step plausible 'because of the broadly structural and contextual character of any considerations that could guide us to native translations of the English cluster of interrelated devices of individuation' (Quine 1969a: 34). Consequently, 'there seem bound to be systematically very different choices, all of which do justice to all dispositions to verbal behaviour on the part of all concerned' (ibid.).

In Section 4 I shall argue that there are not the systematically different choices Quine thinks there seem bound to be. I shall concentrate on rather simple, but obviously central, cases of the *gavagai* kind. My aim is not to deny that there are no *instances* of inscrutability of extension for the predicates of a language, including predicates of our own language English. It is rather to deny that there is the gross degree of inscrutability which Quine claims to have established, and which many philosophers take him to have established, by reflecting on the relations between predicates and the grammatical machinery used in individuation. The conclusion I shall draw is that Quine has failed to show that there is not the determinate relation of reference assumed by the realist. There might be no fact of the matter as regards the relation for some *particular* term, but to establish this one needs to make an empirical investigation of the sort used by Quine in his discussion of the Japanese classifiers and the referents of numerical expressions.

In arguing thus I shall accept Quine's stricture that there is nothing more to guide us in translating or understanding a person's language than the facts about his behaviour and dispositions to behave. In Chapter 3, I shall argue that Quine overlooks, in his purview of translation, non-behavioural physical facts which might give us reason for preferring one translation to another. For the present, however, I shall confine my discussion to the behavioural. I shall also follow Quine in rejecting the myth of a museum. That is, I shall agree that for us to accept one translation or interpretation rather than another, there has to be a behavioural fact of the matter. The whole problem is to be precise about what these facts are.

26

The arguments I shall put forward derive support from some remarks contained in a paper by Gareth Evans (1975). What Evans draws attention to is the fact that identity, and the whole notion of individuation, are in a strong sense secondary to predication from the point of view of a conceptual understanding of language. This suggests there is much more factual information than is considered by Quine. He is thus led to conclude that at least the predicates of our *own* language are not inscrutable; they do bear a determinate relation to the world. In the next section we shall see in what sense Evans thinks predication is a prior notion.

3 IDENTITY AND PREDICATION

Evans's primary concern is with whether or not Quine has succeeded in showing, via the *gavagai* and rabbit examples, that there is what he calls 'indeterminacy in the theory of meaning'. That is, he is concerned with Quine's claim to have shown, by developing his argument from radical translation, that in any language, every predicate that divides its extension does so inscrutably. To this end he concentrates on certain primitive languages which may be said to constitute fragments of English.

'It is a quarrelsome man', says Evans, 'who would bicker with Quine over the indeterminacy of translation – the constraints upon that enterprise being so slight' (1975: 344). It is far from clear, however, that the constraints on translation are so slight. In passing I mentioned Quine's availing himself of N. L. Wilson's 'principle of charity' in order to avoid attributing absurdity to another's behaviour. It amounts to assuming that the beliefs of others, including foreigners, are much the same as our own in many commonplace matters. But belief is perhaps too shallow a category on its own. If our aim is to understand the behaviour, both verbal and physical, of a member of some linguistic community, then it seems that what is required is not just a theory of *translation* but a theory of *interpretation*. We need to interpret actions – gestures, behaviour when prompted, etc. – before we can translate sentences. Both Davidson (1973*a*) and Lewis (1974) have suggested that interpretation in this way underlies translation. Clearly enough, a theory of interpretation requires a theory of action. Now in order to explain why a person acted in the way he did, it is not sufficient simply to attribute certain beliefs to him, for example, beliefs about the outcome of his action; we also

27

need to identify the desires he has – why he wanted that outcome in the first place. Thus Richard Grandy recommends a more generous principle:

If a translation tells us that the other person's beliefs and desires are connected in a way that is too bizarre for us to make sense of, then the translation is useless for our purposes. So we have, as a pragmatic constraint on translation, the condition that the imputed pattern of relations among beliefs, desires and the world be as similar to our own as possible. This principle I shall call the *principle of humanity*. (1973: 443)

Lewis goes further still and suggests an additional five principles. I shall discuss the matter again in Chapter 3.

Returning to Evans's article, it is clear that when he talks of indeterminacy he means that which might result from the inscrutability of foreign terms. As indicated already in this chapter, on this point I too am one of those who would bicker with Quine. By drawing attention to certain features of the structure and function of our own language, Evans presents strong reasons for rejecting Quine's claim to have shown inscrutability in the concept of reference. In the next section I shall build on Evans's insight and offer a general argument against inscrutability both at home *and* as it affects our translation of a foreign language of the sort Quine considers. Not only is reference a determinate relation at home, it also makes sense to see it as determinate for a foreign language.

To begin with, Evans points out that Quine's argument for inscrutability rests upon the belief that, 'the sole reason a semanticist can have for treating an expression as a predicate with a particular divided reference is to account for that expression's interaction with the (putative) apparatus of individuation' (1975: 345–6). We encountered this reason most recently in the passage quoted towards the end of the last section which, I said, constitutes the vital step in Quine's examples. It originally arose in the context of Quine's explanation of 'analytical hypotheses'. Evans maintains that this reason is mistaken on two counts. To begin with, the 'empirical location of the scheme of predication' is really to be identified by quite different means from its interaction with the apparatus of individuation. Furthermore, this apparatus itself only succeeds in locating the scheme because it is fixed in turn by these other means. Let us look at the first count in detail.

In a way reminiscent of some of Dummett's remarks on truth (Dummett 1958), Evans argues that before we talk about reference we first have to be clear about the *point* of construing an expression, "G", as a predicate which divides its reference over, say, rabbits and not rabbit parts or the like. The point is:

To explain how the truth conditions of certain elementary, but compound, sentences into which it enters are determined by their parts . . . To see the notion "what G is a predicate of" in this way is to see it as constrained by a theory of sentence composition into which it fits and which alone gives it sense. (Evans 1975: 346)

Only in this way, he says, can the semantic theorist do justice to Davidson's insight that a learnable language must have a finite theory of meaning (Evans 1975: 343–4). Given this view about the point of interpreting a predicate in a particular way, the apparatus of individuation is indeed secondary. As an extreme case – discussed further in the next paragraph – we can imagine it being absent from a set of elementary sentences of the form "*Fx*", where "*F*" is some predicate and "*x*" is a free variable. It will also no longer seem surprising that the notion "what G is a predicate of" should then be underdetermined by data exclusively derived from the assent conditions of laconic one-word utterances, like "*Gavagai*", and of sentences putatively involving interaction with the apparatus of individuation, like "*Ip gavagai bleg op gavagai*", 'for by concentrating upon such data we thereby disregard precisely those compound sentences which give the notion its point' (Evans 1975: 346).

What are the compound sentences that give the notion its point? By way of example, Evans asks us to consider a simple language in which the apparatus of individuation – plurals, pronouns, numerals, the identity predicate, the definite article – plays no part. This language contains expressions G_1, G_2, . . . , G_n which, as one-word occasion sentences, we can establish as stimulus synonymous with our "A rabbit!" (and hence with our "A rabbit part!" and "A rabbit stage!"), "A man!", and so on. It also contains expressions F_1, F_2, . . . , F_n which, when queried, are assented to when the environment manifests the presence of certain general features that do not require the presence of a specific kind of object. They are stimulus synonymous with our "White!", "Furry!", "Warm!", "Blood-stained!", and so on. These expressions stand alone as occasion sentences and also with a sentential negation operator. (Quine accepts that we can determinately translate the negation operator (1960: section 13).) It is also observed that complex sentences are

29

formed by combining one of the F terms with one of the G terms, although two G terms are never coupled together. Furthermore, the negation operator is also found to occur with the F terms to yield an internal negation, (not-F G), which is syntactically and behaviourally distinguishable from the external negation Not-(F G).

Evans then argues that the assent conditions for (F G), for example, for "White rabbit", may well turn out to be such that the F feature has to be distributed 'in a characteristic way in relation to the boundaries of a *single* object whose presence prompts assent to the queried G terms' (1975: 351). Neither assent to both F and G nor an overlap between the features associated with F and G is sufficient for assent to (F G). Also, in those cases where overlap is sufficient, as in "Bloodstained rabbit", the assent conditions of the internally negated sentence (not-F G), 'again show a sensitivity to the boundaries of an object, for assent requires the *absence* of the associated feature from the entire exposed surface of that object' (ibid.).

How are we to give a systematic account of the truth conditions of these and similar compound sentences? According to Evans, we first have to attribute to the parts of those sentences properties consistent with their occurrences in all other contexts, and then characterize the construction of those sentences in such a way that the truth conditions can be deduced. In Section 2 of his paper, Evans explains in some detail what an acceptable account would look like. As is to be expected, it entails that "rabbit" is to be interpreted as a predicate which divides its extension over rabbits. In Section 3, he argues that none of Quine's alternative semantic proposals are acceptable. Let me briefly summarize Evans's own account.

In so far as we are interested in constructing a theory of meaning for the simple language envisaged, we are obliged to state, among other things, how "White" occurs in "not-White"; the two expressions are clearly not associated with independent conditions. Suppose that the behavioural evidence warrants this general principle for generating the semantical contribution of "not"-φ from that of φ: an object satisfies "not"-φ if and only if the object does not satisfy φ. Then it follows that contradiction will result if both predicates are applied to the same object. So the distribution of whiteness throughout a rabbit-shaped area and not some other is relevant to the judgments "White rabbit" and "not-White rabbit", 'precisely because either judgment affirmed upon an insufficiently extended survey is liable to be *contradicted* by the other judgment, warranted by the condition of, and made with respect to, the same rabbit' (Evans 1975: 352).

Here we touch upon what Evans calls 'the deep connection' between predication and identity, and thus upon the rest of the apparatus of individuation. At this point, too, Evans makes clear the second count on which he thinks Quine's 'sole reason' is mistaken. A necessary condition for a predicate to be the identity predicate is that the way speakers use sentences containing it reveals a disposition to withhold contradictory predicates from the things identified. Now there might well be cases where, because of the structure of the sentences of a language, we are forced, in giving a theory of meaning for the language, to recognize predication without also identifying an identity predicate. But for any language at all, we could never recognize an identity sentence save by its inferential connections to such predicative sentences; in particular, its use in conformity with the principle of the non-identity of discernibles. Of course then, Quine was right to find the identification of the identity predicate undetermined by the data he considered, for upon such a basis one could not show that an expression behaves in the required way in relation to contradictory predicates. But this underdetermination is relatively unimportant once we appreciate that identity has to be tied to the rest of the language. As Evans concludes, 'we may suppose that what objects a language distinguishes and talks about is a matter embedded much deeper than Quine's talk of jiggling with the translation of the individuative apparatus would lead us to believe' (1975: 353).

This is as far as I wish to take the discussion of Evans's article. The line of his central argument should now be clear. The point of construing a predicate of a language as having a particular extension is to explain how the truth conditions of whole sentences of the language come to be determined by the references of their parts. We need to be able to explain this in order to satisfy the requirement that a learnable language has a finite theory of meaning. How to construe a predicate is what we focus on when we look at the interrelations between, say, the negation operator and certain categories of expressions in the language. We are then seeking a systematic account of how the truth conditions of those sentences depend on their structure. This account requires conformity with certain principles of identity, but these are only recognized from the way in which the predicates of the language are themselves used. So explaining the scheme of predication of a language by considering the available behavioural evidence is epistemologically prior to investigating how predicates interact with the individuative apparatus. Thus, we can explain the truth conditions of compound sentences of, say, the form $(F\ G)$ and $(\text{not-}F\ G)$, given our recognition of their sensitivity to the identity conditions of rabbits, by suggesting that the sentences involve predicates of rabbits.

How successful is Evans in replying to Quine's claims to have shown that there is inscrutability in the theory of reference? By drawing attention to certain features of the structure of our language and the way it functions, Evans is able to point to a mass of detail which has to be accounted for when we contemplate constructing a theory of meaning for our language. The onus is surely on Quine to explain how his alternative proposals account for it in an equally satisfactory way. True enough, we have not looked at Evans's arguments against the possibility of such a Quinean retort. There are two reasons for this. The first is that my main purpose in relating Evans's proposals is to be able to draw upon them in the next section when I present my own arguments against inscrutability. The second is that, by replying to Quine's alternative proposals myself in the next section, the need for explaining Evans's replies is obviated.

As was noted at the beginning of this section, Evans sees little point in replying to the argument for inscrutability as it arises in translation from a foreign language. Thus he confines his attention to fragments of English, whose sentences have structures and assent conditions familiar to us. The 'simple language' we considered was only a small fragment. In attempting to display shortcomings in Quine's semantic proposals, the fragments are considerably larger. Obviously, the larger the fragment the less the arguments can be expected to carry over to the area of radical translation.

In the next section I shall be concentrating not on fragments of English, but on the domain of language Quine takes as the background for radical translation. My argument will be in four stages. I shall begin by making some further remarks about the structure of sentences containing the negation operator. The way in which the negation operator interacts with predicates will be contrasted with the way in which it interacts with singular terms. I shall then argue that the structural differences revealed in this way, together with other criteria if necessary, suggest a general way in which a linguist might identify a category of terms in a foreign language as corresponding to the category of singular terms in the home language, and thus refute an argument of Quine's against the possibility of such an identification. In the second stage I shall maintain that, having identified this category, the linguist will then be able to recognize the foreign quantifier construction, which in turn will enable him to recognize logical similarities between the two languages. Given what Evans has said about the relations between identity and predication, together with one or two further remarks, it will be argued in the third stage that no reason so far given by Quine shows that the linguist will not be in a position to *translate uniquely* the predicate which he at first naively takes to be that of identity. As we have seen, both in this section and the last, once this is fixed so are the translations of the predicates. This will be clarified in the final stage.

It must be emphasized that I am not going to give some kind of generalization of Evans's argument. Evans places no weight on the reasons which a person constructing a theory of meaning might have for identifying certain expressions as singular terms. As I have remarked, however, my arguments will have just as much bearing on the case where a linguist is trying to construct a translation manual for an alien language. Thus it should not be surprising that I shall have to take into account evidence relating to other categories of expressions. Moreover, I shall seek to show that, given the close connection between singular terms and quantifiers, it is to be expected that the category of expression which is of particular significance is that of singular terms.

4 HOW TO CATCH *GAVAGAI*

Quine has contrasted the way in which we can translate foreign predicates and quantifiers with the way in which we translate the truth functions. The latter is facilitated by the fact that we can state 'substantial behavioural conditions' for interpreting foreign operators like negation and alternation (1969b: 103; 1960: Section 13). When it comes to quantified sentences, however, matters stand differently, for they 'depend for their truth on the objects . . . of which the component terms are true; and what those objects are is not uniquely determined by stimulus meaning. Indeed . . . like plural endings and identity [they] are part of our own special apparatus of objective reference' (1960: 61). Moreover, we shall first need to decide which foreign terms correspond to our predicates and which to our singular terms. (Of course, if there are no such classes of terms in the foreign language then there is no correspondence, but then nor will there be inscrutability.) According to Quine, however, even the distinction between predicates and singular terms is independent of stimulus meaning. I wish to begin by challenging this last claim.

In pursuing an inductive definition of the class of foreign sentences, a linguist will have recognized certain large classes of expressions which might be termed 'grammatical categories'. Will he have any reason to correlate one of these categories with our English category of singular terms? The problem he faces, says Quine, is similar to that involved in deciding on the extension of an expression like "*gavagai*". Thus, the singular term "Bernard J. Ortcutt" 'differs none in stimulus meaning from a general term true of each of the good dean's temporal segments, and none from a general term true of each of his spatial parts' (Quine 1960: 52). The only way to decide is by appeal to the apparatus of individuation. But is this in fact the case? What Quine is saying is that for a unique translation to be made the linguist has to accept one or more analytical hypotheses, for no appeal to the behavioural facts is in itself sufficient. Let us consider more closely, then, what some of these facts are.

To begin with, the linguist will be able to glean quite a lot of information by reflecting on the different ways in which singular terms and predicates interact with the negation operator. The difference is encapsulated in Aristotle's dictum that a quality has a contrary but a substance does not. This may be interpreted in the following way. To say that a quality has a contrary is to say that, for any predicate "*F*" there is another predicate "not-*F*" which is true of just those objects of which the original predicate is false, and false of just those objects of which the original predicate is true. To say that a substance does not have a contrary is to say that we cannot in general assume that, for any given object *a*, there is some object *b*, distinct from *a*, of which just those predicates which are false of *a* are true of *b*, and just those which are false of *b* are true of *a*.

The fact that qualities have contraries but objects lack them is of particular importance to the linguist. It is revealed in natural language by a speaker's acceptance, as equally grammatical, of the expression "not-*F*" in any context containing "*F*", together with his refusal to recognize the use of an expression of the form "not-*a*". For a speaker who uses "Bernard J. Ortcutt" as a name, and hence as a singular term, the expression "not-Bernard J. Ortcutt" is nonsensical. Consequently, the repeated use by an inquisitive linguist of "not-a_1", where "a_1" is a foreign name, in attempting to produce a statement is always likely to result not so much in refusal to assent or dissent on the part of a native speaker, but in his expressing bewilderment. It is another matter when negation of a predicate is the putative issue. If the linguist thinks he can also identify a foreign predicate "F_1", then his repeated prompting of the native speaker with ("not"-F_1 a_1) should sometimes elicit *either* assent or dissent. Notice too that in talking of the expression of bewilderment – an amazed look, a boggle – and the refusal to assent or dissent – a shrug, a gesture – we are dealing with features that are behaviourally detectable. Also, factual surprise or mere indifference in response to a grammatical sentence will not always occur; syntactic bewilderment in response to a non-grammatical sentence always will.

The above remarks suggest the following guideline which might be used by a behaviourally conscious linguist in translating a foreign language:

(A) For any (putative) singular term "a" and predicate "F" of a foreign language, if a user of that language either assents to or dissents from the sentence "Fa", then he will usually express bewilderment when confronted by sequences of phonemes containing the expression "not"-a, and will (thus) invariably refuse to assent to or dissent from them, though he will invariably either assent to or dissent from the sentence ("not"-F a).

Given his recognition that there are foreign grammatical categories, I submit that, on the basis of a sufficiently wide survey of the behavioural evidence, the linguist will be able to use (A) alone in order to settle on the foreign category most similar to our category of singular terms. It certainly decides the issue for the "Bernard J. Ortcutt" example, and since this is Quine's *only* direct argument against the possibility of deciding on the class of singular terms, I conclude that he has failed to prove that the distinction between predicates and singular terms is independent of stimulus meaning.

We should further note that (A) is not the only guideline a linguist can use in attempting to detect singular terms. Leaving aside the foreigner's reaction to certain sequences of phonemes containing the negation operator, suppose we look at those cases where he refuses either to assent to or dissent from an utterance which the linguist has good reason to believe is a member of the class of foreign sentences. It has been claimed by Strawson (1969: 100), and accepted by Quine (1969d: 320–1), that this reflects a truth-value gap, i.e., a sentence which is neither true nor false. This might not always be the case. It might be, for example, that assent or dissent would amount to a flagrant disregard for some social convention on the part of a speaker. Let us suppose, however, that such difficulties could be resolved by sufficiently varying the circumstances of the questioning.

Strawson goes on to point out that, 'whether the sentence is true or false depends on the success or failure of the general term; but the failure of the singular term appears to deprive the general term of the chance of either success or failure' (1969: 100). This would seem to suggest, and Strawson certainly writes as though it suggests, that truth-value gaps will be seen to depend systematically on members of one grammatical category. Replying to Strawson, Quine claims that, 'there will of course be the problem of deciding which word of the truth-valueless sentence to blame the truth-value gap on, and there will be other technical problems' (1969d: 321). Unfortunately Quine does not elaborate on what these 'technical problems' might be. The problem of 'which word' seems to have more substance to it. Truth-value gaps arise in our own language for a variety of reasons other than failure of reference on the part of a singular term: category mistakes, presuppositions, ambiguity, vagueness, and the like. Can these be overcome by casting the net in search of evidence sufficiently wide? Surely we need to emphasize the empirical spirit here. And what is more, the linguist should be able, with the help of (A), to check any hypothesis he may be led to form.

Another guideline is suggested by the evidence that can be deduced from reflecting on how singular terms interact with the category of predicates. In our own language, we never find a person assenting to, say, "F_1 Ortcutt" and "F_2 Ortcutt" without being prepared to assent to the compound "$F_1 F_2$ Ortcutt". Could the linguist use this as a further aid in translation? It would be a bizarre language indeed where a speaker assented to some object having property F_1 and to the same object having property F_2, while refusing to assent to that object having both F_1 and F_2. As for the problem of identifying the foreign category of predicates, guideline (A) will be of help here. Notice also that such an aid casts further doubt on

Quine's original argument against identifying foreign singular terms. If "Ortcutt" were treated as a predicate true of several things, then the aid could be preserved upon one assumption only: that whatever is true of one Ortcutt is true of all. That is, if the principle is to hold, then the linguist can only regard what are putatively singular terms as predicates on the assumption that the several things of which the term is true are indiscernible by the predicates with which it interacts. This seems implausible.

As a final guideline to the establishment of some foreign category as the category of singular terms, let us once more look at how the negation operator functions in elementary sentences. Suppose that a speaker of the foreign language that our linguist is trying to translate assents to a sentence that the linguist takes to be of the form "Not"-(Fa), where "a" is a referring singular term. He can check whether this is the form by seeing if the speaker also assents to ("not"-F a). For if a person is disposed to assent to its not being the case that a is F, and given that there is something to which "a" refers, it would seem that he should be equally disposed to assent to its being the case that a is not-F (and vice-versa). Or at any rate, if someone maintains that a person might not be equally disposed, it is surely incumbent upon them to explain how the difference could be manifested via a speaker's dispositions to assent and dissent. The same points may be made *mutatis mutandis* for the case where the speaker dissents from "Not"-(Fa). This suggests the following guideline for translation:

(B) For any (putative) referring singular term "a" and predicate "F" of a foreign language, a speaker's dispositions to assent to or dissent from "Not"-(Fa) are the same as his dispositions to assent to or dissent from ("not"-F a).

This completes the first stage of my argument against the inscrutability of reference. I have put forward several guidelines for helping the linguist decide which foreign grammatical category is most similar to our own category of singular terms. Each of them sought to exploit certain facts about the structure of natural language. The first enabled us to rebut Quine's contrary argument and I suggested that it offered sufficient evidence in itself for a decision to be made. I then suggested three other guidelines, of varying strengths, to which the linguist might also appeal. The second of these provided a further argument against Quine's claim. At no point in the discussion did I assume that the linguist requires more than the behavioural evidence for putting these guidelines into practice. There was no need to; the behavioural evidence itself is overwhelming.

The second stage of the argument concerns how the linguist is to recognize the foreign quantifier construction. This is not the same thing as translating sentences of the foreign language containing quantifiers. For that we have to know, as Quine says, which things count as objects in the foreign language. How then does the linguist recognize quantification?

One answer emerges when Quine reflects on substitutional quantification:

> Behavioural conditions for interpreting a native construction as existential substitutional quantification, then, are readily formulated. We fix on parts of the construction as candidates for the roles of quantifier and variable; then a condition of their fitness is that the natives be disposed to dissent from a whole quantified sentence when and only when disposed to dissent from each of the sentences obtainable by dropping the quantifier and substituting for the variable. A second condition is that the natives be disposed to assent to one of the sentences obtainable by dropping the quantifier and substituting for the variable. (1969b: 104–5)

This might seem to be a rather haphazard procedure since for any one choice of native expressions as candidates for the role of quantifier and variable, an infinite lot of quantified sentences and substitution instances would have to be tested. But Quine's faith in the empirical method is great; he believes empirical induction to be all we should require (ibid.).

There are as many kinds of substitutional quantification for a language as there are admissible substitution classes. Since the linguist is now able to recognize the foreign category of singular terms, however, let us focus on it as the substitution class. As Christopher Hill has pointed out (1971: 71), the experiments described by Quine will sometimes indicate that the foreigners are using objectual, or referential, quantifiers. For if there is at least one existentially quantified sentence which commands assent, while each of its substitution instances tends to provoke dissent, the foreigners will be counted referentialists, believers in nameless objects. Hill goes on:

> On the other hand, when informants are found assenting and dissenting as Quine describes, their quantifiers can be viewed either way. Certainly they could be substitutional quantifiers. It is possible, though, that the natives have an ontology which is bigger than their stock of names, but that no predicate of their theory is satisfied by just the nameless objects. Since both hypotheses accord equally well with patterns of assent and dissent, Quine

says that they come to the same thing: in this situation, he is unable 'to distinguish objectively between referential quantification and a substitutional counterfeit'. (1971: 71)

More recently, Quine has expressed some doubt about the claimed inability to distinguish (1974: 326–7), but the intricacies of the argument need not concern us here. What is important to us is Quine's acknowledgment that there is a point to the question of whether a given foreign expression counts as an existential quantifier. The linguist can now add to his previous knowledge of the foreign truth-functions. He will be able to map foreign sentences onto those classes of English sentences which have the same logical form up to the level where substitutional and referential quantification diverge. To use a phrase of Hill's, the linguist will be in a position to recognize 'logical similarities' between the two languages.

We now come to the crucial third stage of the argument, where we need to bear in mind what Evans calls 'the deep connection' between identity and predication. The linguist would like to be able to decide whether a particular foreign two-place predicate, say *"bleg"*, can be translated by our identity sign. What Evans's remarks show is that there is at least *one* criterion for deciding. This criterion is that the way speakers of the language use sentences containing *"bleg"* must reveal a disposition to withhold contradictory predicates from the things identified; they must use it in conformity with the principle of the non-identity of discernibles. We may formulate this principle as:

(ND) $(x)(y) [(Fx \mathbin{\&} {\sim}Fy) \supset {\sim}(x = y)]$

It is easily proved that (ND) is interderivable in first-order logic with the principle of the indiscernibility of identicals:

(II) $(x)(y) [(x = y \mathbin{\&} Fx) \supset Fy]$

Now in order to generate all the valid schemata of the logic of identity, given first-order logic, the axiom-schema (II) needs to be supplemented by the axiom-schema:

(I) $(x) (x = x)$

This suggests a further criterion for deciding whether a foreign predicate corresponds to our identity predicate: speakers of the foreign language must show a disposition to assent to statements of self-identity.

To check whether the foreign two-place predicate *"bleg"* is in fact

39

the same as our identity predicate, the linguist can obtain what would in that case be instances of the axioms by using what he has established to be foreign singular terms When a foreigner is found assenting to a sentence containing "*bleg*" and two singular terms "a_1" and "a_2", and to a sentence containing "a_1" (or "a_2") in one or more of its argument places, then he must be disposed to assent to a third sentence of exactly the same form as the second but which has "a_2" (or "a_1") substituted one or more times for "a_1" (or "a_2"). Furthermore, for any foreign singular term "a", a speaker must be disposed to assent to the sentence formed by substituting "a" in both argument places of a sentence containing "*bleg*". It would seem, then, that even within the Quinean strictures on translation, a linguist will be able to determine whether a foreign people share our concept of identity.

We now come to the fourth and final stage of the argument, where the linguist attempts to resolve the translation of "*gavagai*". In Section 1 we saw that when the linguist uses a foreign expression like "*bleg*" in an attempt to decide whether this *gavagai* is the same as that one, it seems that he has no way of telling, without recourse to voluntarily added maxims, whether he is thereby asking about wholes, parts or stages. But having established (*a*) what to count as foreign singular terms, (*b*) logical similarities between the two languages, and (*c*) criteria for when to translate a foreign predicate as an identity predicate, it now seems that the problem will yield to research. Thus, suppose he is worried about whether he has asked if this undetached rabbit part is identical with that undetached rabbit part, rather than whether this rabbit is identical with that one. Then he will proceed as follows. To begin with he obtains a variegated animal, for example one with a white leg and the rest brown, or one to which he adds some dye on an appropriate part. Let us suppose he is lucky and finds a rabbit with a white leg. In the usual way he establishes which foreign word is stimulus synonymous with our "white"; imagine the word is "*fisp*". On the basis of his knowledge of the logical similarities, the linguist then produces the foreign sentence most similar to:

(i) $(\exists x)\,(\exists y)\,(Gx \,\&\, Gy \,\&\, Fx \,\&\, {\sim}Fy \,\&\, Bxy)$

where G is "*gavagai*", F is "*fisp*" and B is "*bleg*" (cf. Hill 1971: 71). Now (i) has the same logical form as both of the following:

(ii) $(\exists x)(\exists y)(Rx \,\&\, Ry \,\&\, Wx \,\&\, {\sim}Wy \,\&\, x = y)$

(iii) $(\exists x)(\exists y)(Ux \& Uy \& Wx \& \sim Wy \& Bxy)$

where R is "rabbit", W is "white", U is "undetached rabbit part" and B is ". . . belongs with ___". The important difference, however, lies in the assent conditions under stimulation in the presence of the variegated rabbit. If the foreigner does assent to (i) then, given the truth of (ND), (ii) would clearly be an incorrect translation. (iii) is the obvious choice. In such a case, it follows not only that *"bleg"* is to be translated as ". . . belongs with ___", but also that *"gavagai"* is a predicate true of undetached parts of rabbits. If, on the other hand, the foreigner dissents from (i) then, of course, (iii) is ruled out as the correct translation. "Rabbit" might be the correct translation of *"gavagai"*, but so might "rabbit stage"; we shall resolve this quandary shortly.

One possible reply to this line of argument would be that *"fisp"* is not a simple predicate like "white", but is a complex predicate meaning something like "white in some place". When it appears twice in one sentence, the place in question is assumed to have changed. The correct translation of (i), it might then be urged, would be:

(ii') $(\exists x)(\exists y)(Rx \& Ry \& Px \& \sim Py \& x = y)$

where R is "rabbit" and P is "white in some place". But even such a perverse hypothesis as this can be tested. If *"fisp"* is really stimulus synonymous with "white in some place", then for anything to be *fisp* there has to be some place in which it is white. That is, *"fisp"* has to be understood as a two-place predicate. So whenever a foreigner assents to its being the case that there is some one thing that is *fisp*, he will also assent to a double instantiation of the form:

(iv) $(\exists x)(\exists y)(Fxy)$

Having resolved the problem about undetached rabbit parts, let us now see how the linguist copes with rabbit stages. The suggestion that the foreign people individuate stages of rabbits rather than persisting rabbits implies that no statement asserting the identity of *gavagais* over time will be true. In order to exploit this fact, our linguist will need to have some way of fixing the times of certain events – certain 'ocular irradiation patterns' as Quine calls them – in a way acceptable to the foreigner. He should encounter little difficulty in this. If the foreigner does indeed individuate stages and talks about them in conformity with a concept of identity, he must be acutely aware of the passage of time. Perhaps the Quinean device of 'properly timed blindfoldings' will allow him to settle on some temporal predications for sightings of *gavagais*. Maybe he will need to avail himself of other events, like a flash of lightning, or the setting of the sun, which he can use to establish a translation of "before". At any rate, there would appear to be numerous alternatives. Let us suppose that he decides the translation of our complex predicate "seen before the lightning flash" is *"ky lan worrat"*. Blending this with *"gavagai"*, *"bleg"*, existential quantifier constructions and a few other logical terms, the linguist produces a sentence which looks like:

(v) $(\exists x)(\exists y)(Gx \text{ \& } Gy \text{ \& } Kx \text{ \& } {\sim}Ky \text{ \& } Bxy)$

where G is *"gavagai"*, K is *"ky lan worrat"* and B is *"bleg"*.

Now (v) has the same logical form as both of the following:

(vi) $(\exists x)(\exists y)(Rx \text{ \& } Ry \text{ \& } Lx \text{ \& } {\sim}Ly \text{ \& } x = y)$

(vii) $(\exists x)(\exists y)(Sx \text{ \& } Sy \text{ \& } Lx \text{ \& } {\sim}Ly \text{ \& } Axy)$

where R is "rabbit", L is "seen before the lightning flash", S is "rabbit stage" and A is ". . . is a stage of the same animal as __". But the difference between (vi) and (vii) is revealed in the same way as the difference between (ii) and (iii), by looking at the assent conditions. In this case, however, the foreigner is not stimulated by the presence of a variegated rabbit, but by the appearance of any one rabbit at different times. If he assents to (v) then, given the truth of (ND), (vii) must be the correct translation. Consequently, the linguist would know to translate *"bleg"* as ". . . is a stage of the same animal as __", and *"gavagai"* as "rabbit stage". Dissent from (v) on the part of the foreigner rules out (vii) as a translation.

Over the last few pages I have been considering how to distinguish a foreign predicate true of rabbits from two perverse alternatives – one true of undetached rabbit parts and one true of temporal stages of rabbits – and how to distinguish the perverse alternatives from each other. I have shown how a cunning linguist can accomplish this by examining the ways in which the foreign predicate interacts with the foreign identity predicate. Where the foreigners are partial to parts and not to wholes or stages, they will assent to a statement, such as (i), to the effect that different parts belong to one and the same object; where they are not partial in this way they would take the statement as not being about parts at all, or as being about different objects.

Where they are partial to stages and not to wholes or parts, the foreigners will invariably assent to a statement, such as (v), according to which the object identified changes with time; otherwise they would sometimes see the same object over time.

The problem does not quite end here. Throughout this chapter I have simplified the discussion by considering as possible translations of "*gavagai*" only those expressions which divide their reference. When presenting the argument for radical translation in *Word and Object*, however, Quine also suggests as two other possible translations "rabbithood" – the universal term – and "the rabbit fusion" – the fusion, in Nelson Goodman's sense, of all rabbits (Quine 1960: 52). The occasion sentence "*Gavagai*" would then be stimulus synonymous with "Rabbithood is manifested here" or "The rabbit fusion is manifested here". What is different about these alternative translations is that they are singular terms and so do not divide their reference at all. Evans considers these possibilities in the article I discussed; we must now do the same.

The obvious reply for us to make is that the guidelines presented at the beginning of this section for distinguishing the category of foreign singular terms will allow the linguist to settle the matter. Thus, there is no contrary of "rabbithood" or "the rabbit fusion". If additional, independent evidence were required, the linguist could obtain it in the following way. Where there is indecision about "rabbit" and "rabbithood", he waits until the object which prompts "*Gavagai*" moves. A predicate is found which applies to its first position but not to its second, and an appropriate variant of (i) is uttered to the foreigner. Assent indicates "rabbithood", since any manifestation of it is a manifestation of the *same* thing, the universal "rabbithood". A similar procedure distinguishes "rabbit" from "the rabbit fusion". Different rabbits have different predicates true of them, but a predicate true of 'that single though discontinuous portion of the spatiotemporal world that consists of rabbits' will not, indeed cannot, vary from rabbit to rabbit. Lastly, if the linguist is not sure whether "rabbithood" or "the rabbit fusion" is intended, he can make use of the fact that a detached part of a rabbit is a part of the discontinuous portion of the spatiotemporal world that consists of rabbits. Such a part is thus an instantiation of the rabbit fusion but obviously not of rabbithood.

In Section 2, I reported an argument of Quine's which purported to show that, because of the inscrutability of reference, there could be not only logically incompatible translation manuals from a foreign language to ours, but also logically incompatible assignments of references or extensions to many expressions of our own language. The leading ideas behind Quine's argument are that the theory of reference for a language – what the extensions of the predicates are and what the singular terms denote – can only be settled by examining the individuative apparatus of that language, and that this is underdetermined by all the behavioural evidence that could be collected because of the evidence's 'broadly structural and contextual character'. In Section 3, I closely examined what Evans thought was wrong with the first idea. Predication, not individuation, is the key notion intimately bound with reference. Individuation is a secondary notion and can only be explained by considering how predicates function in language. Evans's own conclusion is that there are not going to be the logically incompatible assignments of extensions to the predicates of our own language that Quine thinks there will be.

In this section I have taken the key points Evans made about identity and predication and shown that inscrutability does not arise in translation from a foreign language in the way predicted by Quine. Clearly, if there is not the predicted inscrutability here then the argument by analogy for inscrutability at home collapses. Throughout the discussion we have not exceeded the bounds that Quine himself imposes on translation. On the basis of the predicted behavioural evidence we were able to refute his claims about the indeterminacy of translating from one grammatical category to another, and even within the grammatical categories of singular term and predicate we were able to resolve indecisions about how to translate the expression "*gavagai*".

All of this said, I do not pretend to have shown that *all* terms, even within our own language, have a scrutable reference. Thus, I have said nothing that directly casts doubt on cases of deferred ostension or on the example of the Japanese classifiers. I have confined my attention to attacking one argument which Quine hopes will establish inscrutability on a grand scale. It might turn out that an ingenious reply will save the purported example. The assumptions I have made about translation in this section, many of which are taken over from Quine to be used *ad hominem*, might be questioned, although they seem perfectly acceptable when construed as statements about how we interpret our own language. In the end, then, the charge stands that Quine's argument from radical translation pays far too little attention to the fine-grained structure of language, to the ways in which singular terms and predicates interact with truth-functions and quantifiers in order to give complex sentences whose truth-values depend on the references of their parts.

At the beginning of Section 2 of this chapter we noted that any statements about the extensions or referents of the expressions of a language are contained in a metalanguage or background language. Quine's argument purports to show that, for a very wide range of expressions, there will be logically incompatible assignments within the one metalanguage, and that there are no behavioural facts which would enable us to decide between them. I have argued that, on the contrary, there are behavioural facts which settle the matter for Quine's main example. So in this case there is a fact of the matter about which assignment is the correct one. My conclusion, therefore, is that Quine's argument fails to show that there is no determinate relation of reference between expressions of a language and parts of the world. In the next two chapters I shall explain what the significance of this relation is for the realist.

3

A theory of interpretation

The third most basic of the four questions I originally posed as being crucial to a realist defence of the growth of scientific knowledge was:

(3) What conditions have to be satisfied by a natural kind predicate "φ" and an object a in order for "φ", as it is used within a linguistic community C, to be correctly applied to a?

I explained that this was a question of conceptual analysis, of what it is for a natural kind predicate to have an extension. In the next chapter I shall consider in detail what the correct answer is to this question. Even at this stage, however, it should be apparent what sort of answer I shall be proposing. I take the theory of reference underlying my realist position to be firmly in the tradition of Frege. The extension of a predicate is thus a function of its sense, and sense is an epistemological notion derivative from belief. I shall explain these ideas more fully in the next chapter. For the present I wish to make clear that, according to the account I shall give, an investigation into which objects belong to the extension of a natural kind predicate "φ", as it is used within a linguistic community C, is first and foremost, though not only, an investigation into what descriptions could be consistently attributed to φs on the basis of what is believed about φs within C. The first task of such an epistemological investigation, then, will be to find out what members of C believe, or believed, about φs.

What information will be available to one engaged on such a task? Apparently this will depend on the nature of the linguistic community whose language he is investigating. In discussing the growth of scientific knowledge, the communities will frequently be ones like "seventeenth-century French chemists", "late nineteenth-century physicists" and "nineteenth-century Mendelian geneticists", i.e., communities previous to our own. In such cases the information will generally be limited to what can be deduced from physical objects which have endured since that time: books, articles, scientific instruments, and so on. For communities not so distant there might also be memories passed on, the "oral tradition" so to speak. The problem faced by the investigator is that of arriving at a characterization of the intentional states – primarily the belief states – of earlier theorists given such limited information.

One way of seeing this attempt to understand previous scientific theories is as a special case of translating from an alien or foreign language. Rather than languages, however, the investigator will adopt as basic previous scientific theories. Beginning with established translations of relatively observational terms, he proceeds to translate the more theoretical ones until he achieves a coherent translation of statements about φs, on the basis of which he is able to impute beliefs about φs to the earlier theorists. What is assumed throughout is that the intentional states are there to be investigated. The realist views them as forming an objective subject–matter, albeit one whose investigation poses difficult methodological problems.

In this chapter I wish to consider the argument of Quine's which aims to show that, given the methodological problems facing a translator, not only is translation *under*determined by all possible evidence, but that there is *no fact of the matter* for the translator to be right or wrong about. Translation is, to use Quine's expression, *in*determinate. The conclusion he draws is that we must adopt a non-realist attitude to intentional states. If he is right, theories of reference of the kind I wish to defend must be rejected.

What does Quine mean when he says that translation is indeterminate? We recall from the preceding chapter that, according to Quine, a speaker's knowledge of a language – the meanings he attaches to his words – is manifested primarily in his dispositions to assent to and dissent from sentences. If we wish to investigate this knowledge we must therefore attach meanings to his words in a way that accords with his verbal dispositions. The result is an interpretation of his words that is expressive of an intelligible belief set. Given this picture of verbal behaviour, Quine says:

manuals for translating one language into another can be set up in divergent ways, all compatible with the totality of speech dispositions, yet incompatible with one another. In countless places they will diverge in giving, as their respective translations of a sentence of the one language, sentences of the other language which stand to each other in no plausible sort of equivalence however loose. (1960: 27)

47

As this formulation of the thesis suggests, Quine adopts the idiom of *radical* translation, i.e., translation from a completely alien language. But as with the *gavagai* example, radical translation is really a strategy for establishing features about our own home language. The translator is then construed as one who is concerned to understand other speakers of a language with which he is familiar. As a fellow speaker he appears to be in a privileged position, for he can resort to homophonic translation and other aids. Quine maintains though that these are merely 'regulative maxims' which help to settle the question of which translation to adopt, not which translation captures the real meanings. The methodological problems are claimed to hold equally for the radical translator and the fellow speaker of English. The thesis may be restated as:

the infinite totality of sentences of any given speaker's language can be so permuted, or mapped onto itself, that (a) the totality of the speaker's dispositions to verbal behaviour remains invariant, and yet (b) the mapping is no mere correlation of sentences with *equivalent* sentences, in any plausible sense of equivalence however loose. (Quine 1960: 27)

So far it might seem that Quine is trying to establish an epistemological point to the effect that all possible observations of verbal behaviour fail to determine a unique interpretation of the sentences of a language. But what makes Quine's whole argument so contentious is that he wishes to make the much stronger ontological or metaphysical point that there is simply no question of one of the interpretations being true and the rest false: 'The point is not that we cannot be sure whether the analytical hypothesis is right, but that there is not even, as there was in the case of [the occasion sentence] "Gavagai", an objective matter to be right or wrong about' (1960: 73). What argument does Quine have to support this conclusion?

As we noted in Chapter 2, what Quine calls 'the real ground' of the doctrine that sentence translation is indeterminate is an inference from the underdetermination of scientific theory by all possible observations. He describes this as follows:

If our physical theory can vary though all possible observations be fixed, then our translation of [a foreigner's] physical theory can vary though our translations of all possible observation reports on his part be fixed. Our translation of his observation sentences no more fixes our translation of his physical theory than our own possible observations fix our own physical theory. (Quine 1970: 179–80)

48

The crucial point, however, is his insistence that the indeterminacy of translation is not just an instance of the empirically underdetermined character of physics. Thus, in an often quoted passage from his reply to Chomsky, Quine says:

> Though linguistics is of course a part of the theory of nature, the indeterminacy of translation is not just inherited as a special case of the underdetermination of our theory of nature. It is parallel but additional. Thus, adopt for now my fully realistic attitude towards electrons and muons and curved space–time, thus falling in with the current theory of the world despite knowing that it is in principle methodologically underdetermined. Consider, from this realistic point of view, the totality of truths of nature, known and unknown, observable and unobservable, past and future. The point about indeterminacy of translation is that it withstands even all this truth, the whole truth about nature. This is what I mean by saying that, where indeterminacy of translation applies, there is no real question of right choice; there is no fact of the matter even to within the acknowledged underdetermination of a theory of nature. (1969c: 303)

This stage of the argument will be discussed at length in the third section of this chapter. Before we come to it, let me make some further clarificatory points.

Despite his calling the argument from underdetermination of theory by evidence 'the real ground' of the doctrine of indeterminacy, Quine nevertheless holds that the *gavagai* example suggests another ground; it presses 'from below'. Since *"Gavagai"* is an observational sentence, it has a stimulus synonymous translation and is itself an example only of the inscrutability of reference of terms, not of the indeterminacy of translation of sentences. To see where it does support indeterminacy, we need to imagine 'that some lengthy non-observational sentences containing *gavagai* could be found which would go into English in materially different ways according as *gavagai* was equated with one or another of the terms "rabbit", "rabbit stage", etc.' (1970: 182). Here we must bear in mind the conclusion of Chapter 2, that even if we accept Quine's stricture that only behavioural facts are relevant in translation, we can establish a unique translation for a predicate such as *gavagai*. It will then be irrelevant whether we are talking about its use in observational or non-observational sentences. For these reasons, I shall confine my attention to the underdetermination of theory by evidence when discussing what argument Quine gives in support of his doctrine of indeterminacy of translation.

The first two stages of the argument Quine calls 'the real ground' are: (i) assume that scientific theory – 'the theory of nature' – is underdetermined by all possible observations; then (ii) it follows that translation is underdetermined by all possible observations. A first query might be raised over the phrase "all possible observations": how, one might ask, could we ever be in a position to rule out all future evidence? But there is a weaker formulation of which Quine can avail himself. There is no reason to think that at any stage of scientific enquiry the totality of observations we have made will force us to accept just one theory; alternatives will always be available.

Increased recognition of the work of Duhem has resulted in general acceptance of this view. Indeed, in most quarters it has come to be regarded as something of a platitude. Now although I think there are interesting questions to be raised about particular purported instances of underdetermination of scientific theory, it does seem that there are numerous examples which are correctly interpreted in this way (Duhem 1954; Newton-Smith 1978). Hence I shall follow the vast majority of Quinean commentators in conceding this first assumption.

Turning now to translation, we need to begin by examining the methodological situation of the radical translator. His aim is to define a function which maps sentences of the alien language onto sentences of the translator's home language. The basic data, as already noted, are the aliens' dispositions to assent to and dissent from sentences, it being assumed that native assent and dissent can be interpreted as such by the translator. In addition to this evidence, Quine thinks there are certain constraints which the translator is methodologically justified in imposing on the function. Observation sentences must be mapped onto sentences of the home language generally assented to in the same circumstances. Truth-functional logic should be imputed to the aliens. Finally, stimulus-analytic (-contradictory) sentences of the alien language should be translated by stimulus-analytic (-contradictory) sentences of the home language. The resultant possible functions Quine, as we noted in the last chapter, calls 'analytical hypotheses'.

Two problems affecting this stage of the argument may be distinguished. The prior one is whether Quine has described the methodological situation correctly. The second is whether, given a correct description, translation is underdetermined by observation. Discussion of the first centres on the issue of what the correct constraints on translation are. Some critics have suggested that Quine is unjustified in imposing the three that he does. Thus Hookway notes, with respect to the third, that the body of stimulus-analytic sentences changes over time, with the result that a sentence like "The sun circles the earth", which may have been stimulus-analytic in the middle ages, is now more likely to be regarded as stimulus-contradictory (1978: 24). The more frequent criticism of Quine, however, is that he ignores other acceptable constraints. I shall consider this criticism in detail in Section 2. The problem of whether, given a correct description of the methodological situation, translation is underdetermined by observation, and the further question of whether translation is indeterminate, will be treated in parallel in the third section.

2 RADICAL TRANSLATION VERSUS RADICAL INTERPRETATION

Quine has frequently drawn attention to the close connections between belief and meaning. In order to determine what sentences of an alien language mean we must decide what beliefs they express. But how can we begin to attribute beliefs without some means of interpreting the language? A start has to be made somewhere, yet any particular point would seem to exceed what is justified by the behavioural facts.

In Chapter 2, I noted one reply to this line of argument which turned on the contrast between a theory of translation and a theory of interpretation. Attention was drawn to the fact that beliefs interact with desires to determine actions. This suggests a way in which the data used to establish translation can be enlarged. In translation the "variables" are belief and meaning; in the interpretation of action they are belief and desire. Perhaps it would be possible to "play off" verbal behaviour and action in such a way as to fix on belief.

Unfortunately it is difficult to see how such a reply could offer real aid, in the form of further constraints, to the radical translator. It is as though instead of having one algebraic equation with two variables he now has two equations with three variables; for a unique solution he needs one more equation with no more variables. Of course, he could impose certain *a priori* restrictions on the plausibility and complexity of the desires ascribable, but any such assumptions about intentional states would seem to beg the question against Quine's

51

argument. For this reason it seems to me that the approaches of Lewis (1974) and Grandy (1973), whereby aliens' beliefs, desires, and world pictures are simply assumed to be as similar to our own as possible, require further clarification. Moreover, as Hookway also notes, even assumptions made about the intentional states of those belonging to the same linguistic community as a translator, assumptions he might intend to impute to the aliens, stand in need of independent support (1978: 27).

A more promising approach to the belief/meaning problem in radical translation is suggested, somewhat ironically, by Quine himself. In his discussion of the translation of sentential connectives, he notes that there will be cases where the translator is obliged to reconstrue the behavioural evidence. This will be so where the implied translations result in assertions which appear to be obviously false. As noted in the previous chapter, he cites approvingly Wilson's 'principle of charity': 'We select as designatum that individual which will make the largest possible number of . . . statements true' (Quine 1960: 59 fn. 2). This principle is so strong that, even in translation at home, 'we will construe a neighbour's word heterophonically now and again if thereby we see our way to making his message less absurd' (Quine 1969a: 46).

Maximizing truth in this way is nothing more than maximizing agreement between speaker and interpreter over particular statements, for the truth of those statements is judged by the latter. The principle of charity, then, is a constraint on translation, one which rests on the idea that speaker and interpreter are to be assumed as sharing certain beliefs. Davidson has recently argued that this principle is the key to overcoming systematic indeterminacy. His claim is that a theory of radical interpretation can, with the aid of the principle, be constructed in a way formally analogous to Tarski's definition of truth. Where he differs from Quine over the principle is in holding that it has to be applied 'across-the-board', not just in connection with the identification of purely sentential connectives. The remainder of this section will be spent examining these views of Davidson's.

Following Quine, Davidson maintains that the crucial notion for a theory of radical interpretation is that of accepting sentences as true. Given the close interrelation of belief and meaning, the only way to then begin interpreting a speaker's words is by assuming general agreement on beliefs:

We get a first approximation to a finished theory by assigning to sentences of a speaker conditions of truth that actually obtain (in our own opinion) just when the speaker holds those sentences true. The guiding policy is to do this as far as possible, subject to considerations of simplicity, hunches about the effects of social conditioning, and of course our common sense, or scientific, knowledge of explicable error. (Davidson 1973c: 19)

Such a procedure 'is not designed to eliminate disagreement, nor can it; its purpose is to make meaningful disagreement possible, and this depends entirely on a foundation – *some* foundation – in agreement' (ibid.). Here we have the basis for a transcendental argument in support of the principle of charity:

Since charity is not an option, but a condition of having a workable theory, it is meaningless to suggest that we might fall into massive error by endorsing it. Until we have successfully established a systematic correlation of sentences held true with sentences held true, there are no mistakes to make. Charity is forced on us; whether we like it or not, if we want to understand others, we must count them right in most matters. If we can produce a theory that reconciles charity and the formal conditions for a theory, we have done all that could be done to ensure communication. Nothing more is possible, and nothing more is needed. (ibid.)

One person to have questioned this argument of Davidson's is Colin McGinn. He claims that an equally good basis for deriving the meanings of sentences held true would be *un*charitably to impute *false* beliefs to a speaker. That is, we would simply suppose that he was repeatedly mistaken and was expressing false beliefs with correspondingly false sentences (McGinn 1977: 523). But this overlooks an important point, for as Davidson says elsewhere:

The methodological advice to interpret in a way that optimizes agreement should not be conceived as resting on a charitable assumption about human intelligence that might turn out to be false. If we cannot find a way to interpret the utterances and other behaviour of a creature as revealing a set of beliefs largely consistent and true by our own standards, we have no reason to count that creature as rational, as having beliefs, or as saying anything. (1973a: 324)

McGinn also draws attention to another argument Davidson has for charity, that before someone can be said to have a belief about something it has to be shown that they have *many* other *true* beliefs about that thing. He rightly points out that this condition is too strong as it stands, for there do seem to be cases where we can justifiably say that a person has a belief about something without his having *many* beliefs about it. Somewhat wide of the mark, though, is

53

McGinn's further point that while possession of a concept requires a certain minimum of true beliefs about members of its extension, so that there cannot be shared concepts without a measure of shared beliefs, this falls short of what Davidson wants, because disagreement concerning an object is then possible unmediated by common concepts with respect to that object (McGinn 1977: 526). To re-fashion an example of Davidson's, what convinces us that some ancients believed *of* the earth that it was flat is that they made a large number of statements which we interpret as true statements concerning the earth and which we take as expressing true beliefs; statements about, for example, the physical shape and climatic conditions of particular parts of its surface. Certainly we have good reason for thinking that they did not share our concept of the earth as a large, cool, solid body circling around a very large, hot star, but as I have emphasized all along, identity of reference is different from identity of sense, and when one talks about 'common concepts' I understand the latter to be the case. If this is so then, contra McGinn, such examples do seem to support Davidson's claim that 'false beliefs tend to undermine the identification of the subject matter; to undermine, therefore, the validity of a description of the belief as being about that subject. And so, in turn, false beliefs undermine the claim that a connected belief is false' (1975: 20–1).

There is also a further, more general argument here which can be brought against McGinn. The consistent aim of attributing false beliefs leads to a radical dissociation of objects, intentional or otherwise, from propositional attitudes. Consider the question "For any predicate 'φ' which is used in a linguistic community C, and any predicate 'ψ' used by us, what are the conditions which a member of C has to satisfy before we can count a perception by him *of* a φ as being a perception *of* a ψ?". McGinn I take to be committed to the view that *no* conditions have to be satisfied. My claim is that he must at least have *some* true beliefs about ψs. This is the absolute minimum which he has to be accorded before we can make any sense of his having a perception at all. A slightly different form of this point will arise in the next chapter when we consider what arguments Saul Kripke has to offer against a certain theory of how the referent of a proper name, or the extension of a natural kind predicate, is fixed.

In the light of these arguments, considerable charity appears to be obligatory on the interpreter. The next question is, how is he to apply it across-the-board? To answer this we need to examine

54

Davidson's theory of radical interpretation more closely. One of his main ideas is that a theory of truth for a language should enable a person to understand any declarative sentence uttered by a speaker of that language. If one knows that when a speaker utters X what he says is true if and only if p, one can grasp what he is claiming to be true, if he is asserting X. It would seem to follow from this that one would be justified in concluding that X means p. But here Davidson says that we have to seriously modify the initial idea that a theory of interpretation is to be based on a theory of truth. Tarski's Convention T demands of a theory of truth that all sentences of which a truth predicate is predicated entail others of a certain form. This gives sentences like the familiar "'Frege died in 1925' is true if and only if Frege died in 1925". Following Davidson, let us call these T-sentences. In Tarski's theory, T-sentences are to be recognized by their syntactic form, but in radical interpretation a syntactical test is not available since it would presuppose an understanding of the language to be interpreted. As Davidson says:

the syntactical test is merely meant to formalize the relation of synonymy or translation, and this relation is taken as unproblematic in Tarski's work on truth. Our outlook inverts Tarski's: we want to achieve an understanding of meaning or translation by assuming a prior grasp of the concept of truth. What we require, therefore, is a way of judging the acceptability of T-sentences that is not syntactical, and makes no use of the concepts of translation, meaning or synonymy, but is such that acceptable T-sentences will in fact yield interpretations. (1974: 318)

Such a way is afforded, according to Davidson, by the principle of charity.

If speakers of a language hold a sentence to be true under certain circumstances observed by the interpreter, then this is to be taken as *prima facie* evidence that the sentence is believed by the speakers to be true under those circumstances. A speaker is thereby assumed to be truthful as far as possible. In this way the interpreter can hope to establish, via numerous positive instances, generalizations like:

$(x)(t)$ (if x is a member of the German linguistic community then (x holds "Es Schneit" true at t if and only if it is snowing near x at t))

which in turn support T-sentences like:

"Es schneit" is true-in-German for a speaker x at time t if and only if it is snowing near x at t.

Here we see an important difference between radical interpretation and radical translation: such reference to objective features of the world which alter in conjunction with changes in attitude towards the truth of sentences replaces Quine's notion of stimulus meaning. Notice also that the appeal to the notion of a linguistic community begs no question, for speakers can be said to belong to the same linguistic community if the same theory of interpretation works for them.

As Davidson is the first to admit, this strategy presents obvious empirical difficulties. Speakers may be wrong about whether it is snowing near them; there will be differences from speaker to speaker, and from time to time for the same speaker, with respect to the circumstances under which a sentence is held true; and so on. Davidson replies by pointing out that a theory of interpretation will have to take account of the holistic nature of a language. This gives another (possibly unintended) sense to his remark that charity has to be applied across-the-board. T-sentences are not to be established one at a time but rather as elements of a pattern which satisfies the formal constraints of a theory of truth. The aim is to get a theory of best fit, although there will be no reason to suppose that there is just one such theory.

This raises the important question of how much indeterminacy there will be in radical interpretation. Before we can assess this we need to look more at the formal constraints. Beginning with those sentences always held true or always held false, i.e., those identified in Quinean radical translation as stimulus-analytic or stimulus-contradictory, and patterns of inference, the radical interpreter looks for the best way to fit his logic, to the extent required to get a theory satisfying Convention T, onto the alien language. Logic is here treated 'as a grid to be fitted onto the language in one fell swoop' (Davidson 1973a: 323). It seems that this will be possible only if he can find, in the alien language, structures of first-order logic required by the theory for the proofs of T-sentences. So every language, if it is to be counted a language at all, will have an underlying logic identical to our own, and this will immensely limit the admissible translations. Identifying connectives, singular terms, predicates, quantifiers, and identity settles matters of logical form. Indexical sentences, whose truth-value is relative to the environment, are interpreted next, in the way outlined two paragraphs ago. Finally, the interpreter tackles those sentences whose truth-value neither commands uniform agreement nor depends systematically on changes in the environment. The hope is that the recursion demanded by the theory will lead to their determinate interpretation.

Despite these remarks, it must be said that Davidson remains vague, perhaps even unsure, about how determinate translation will be. He comments:

There may, as Quine has pointed out in his discussions of ontological relativity, remain room for alternative ontologies, and so for alternative systems for interpreting the predicates of the object language. I believe the range of acceptable theories of truth can be reduced to the point where all acceptable theories will yield T-sentences that we can treat as giving correct interpretations, by application of further reasonable and non-question-begging constraints. But the details must be reserved for another occasion. (1974: 319–20)

So far the occasion appears not to have presented itself. In the next section I shall question Davidson's concession to Quine here and propose several 'non-question-begging constraints', some of which are particularly relevant when it comes to interpreting previous scientific theories. I shall also consider other objections to Davidson's strategy and finish with a recommendation about how we should view translation. Before doing so, though, let me briefly summarize the argument of the chapter up to this point.

Quine maintains that, both in radical translation and in translation of our own home language, it is possible to establish, given all the behavioural evidence, incompatible translation manuals which 'stand to each other in no plausible sort of equivalence however loose'. His argument for this view depends on physical theory being underdetermined by evidence. He admits that some sentences (the observational ones), and the logical connectives, will be determinately translatable, but denies that there is any path leading from them to determinate translations of more theoretical sentences. Moreover, given the interdependence of belief and meaning, there will be no way of ascribing beliefs to speakers or meanings to their words. One is then invited to conclude that there is no fact of the matter about correct translation. If Quine is right, and if indeterminacy implies inscrutability, then severe limitations are imposed on any attempt to discover, in the way suggested here, the extensions of terms from previous scientific theories.

Davidson, broadening the scope of the enquiry from translation of language to interpretation of behaviour and extending some of Quine's earlier remarks, argues that there are certain assumptions that must be made if we are to be able to interpret a language at all. It must have quantification theory as a base, and the speakers of the language must be assumed to be right as often as plausibly possible. The latter assumption solves the problem of the interdependence of belief and meaning by holding belief constant as far as possible while solving for meaning. The former assumption paves the way for modelling a theory of interpretation on a theory of truth. In conjunction with such a model, the assumptions so constrict the possible translation manuals that, far from standing to each other 'in no plausible sort of equivalence however loose', the only indeterminacy is that which affects the predicates.

3 HOW DETERMINATE IS INTERPRETATION?

Since Davidson's theory of radical interpretation is intended as a reply to a doctrine of Quine's, a good place to begin criticism of the theory would be with what Quine has to say about it. Fortunately, Quine has published some comments on Davidson's proposals (1974). He pronounces himself in agreement with the strategy of taking the theory of truth as basic, and appears well disposed, if empirically sceptical, about applying charity across-the-board as a means of disentangling belief and meaning. Despite this, he still foresees two areas where indeterminacy will arise.

The first of these involves inscrutability of reference. Quine agrees with Davidson that Tarski's truth construction cannot be carried through until it is decided what to count as quantification, or the equivalent referential apparatus, in the object language, but points out that in *Word and Object* he argued that such decisions depend on analytical hypotheses and so are not unique. He confesses, though, as we noted in Chapter 2, that recent reflection on substitutional quantification has made him more tentative on this point, 'so maybe one should be more hopeful about the near-uniqueness of the manual up to the point where the truth definition can be brought to bear' (1974: 326). None of this is said to impugn ontological relativity, however, since the values of the variables are not fixed by decisions about quantifiers. What is more, one can have different Tarskian truth definitions, delivering the same totality of expressions as true, yet differing in values assigned to variables. According to Quine, then, inscrutability of reference threatens even in the theory or radical interpretation.

In Chapter 2, I discussed at length Quine's arguments concerning the inscrutability of reference, and the conclusions drawn may now be advanced to support Davidson's position. To begin with, I gave, at the beginning of Section 4 of that chapter, several guidelines which could be used by the radical translator to deduce which alien expressions, if any, correspond to our singular terms. I then explained how he could apply this information, together with that suggested by some of Quine's reflections on substitutional quantification, in a way that would allow him to preserve logical form in translation. And this is exactly what Davidson requires, given his initial assumptions, in order for the first part of his proposed construction of the theory of truth for the alien language to go through. Quine rightly points out that even though we might have to assume that the alien language has quantification theory as a base Davidson has given no explanation of how to decide which alien expressions count as quantifiers. Chapter 2, however, does contain such an explanation.

The third stage of the argument in Chapter 2 made use of some arguments of Evans's which emphasized the deep connection between identity and predication. They suggested how, given the translator's newly acquired knowledge of logical form in the alien language, it would be possible to determine whether or not the alien identity predicate is to be translated by our identity predicate. Then, in the final stage, it was shown how to resolve the quandary over translating the predicate *gavagai*. Furthermore, it was pointed out that at no stage of the argument is it necessary to assume the translator has anything other than behavioural evidence with which to work. He can accept this restriction and still find nothing relative about the alien ontology. We can therefore meet Quine's first objection to Davidson's proposals, as well as ease Davidson's own conscience on the matter.

His second objection relates to the later stages of the construction of a theory of truth for an alien language. While conceding that we can settle the truth of the T-sentence for "Es schneit" as well as we can settle the translation of "Es schneit" into "It's snowing", Quine thinks that 'when we get off to sentences remote from observationality we're going to have the problem of indeterminacy of translation' (1974: 328). Clearly the issue here is the underdetermination of theory by evidence. Allowing for determinate translation of what, for the sake of argument, we might agree to call observational sentences, Quine is claiming that translation of non-observational

59

sentences still remains indeterminate – there is no fact of the matter about it.

In reply, Davidson concedes that indeterminacy will probably enter here, but he thinks the formal constraints imposed by a theory of interpretation will keep it to a minimum. The idea underlying this claim is best expressed in the following passage:

> If we consider any one T-sentence, this proposal [that T-sentences should be true] requires only that if a true sentence is described as true, then its truth conditions are given by some true sentence. But when we consider the constraining need to match truth with truth throughout the language, we realize that any theory acceptable by this standard may yield, in effect, a usable translation manual running from object language to metalanguage. The desired effect is standard in theory building: to extract a rich concept (here something reasonably close to translation) from thin little bits of evidence (here the truth values of sentences) by imposing a formal structure on enough bits. (Davidson 1973*b*: 84)

The formal structure is determined by the fact that any adequate theory of truth based on the Tarskian paradigm has to be finitely axiomatizable and satisfy Convention T. It follows from this that the theory will be recursive. Apparently, then, Davidson's hope is that if we attend to enough 'thin little bits of evidence' we shall be able to translate more and more complex sentences.

These remarks are brief and highly speculative. In the first place we have to distinguish between complex sentences and non-observational sentences. One can generate arbitrarily complex sentences using sentential connectives and observational sentences, but there is no guarantee that these will somehow give the totality of the more theoretical sentences. Davidson's position needs supplementing here: how are we to get from the 'bits of evidence' to the 'rich concept'?

A promising approach is suggested, again somewhat ironically, by taking seriously the Duhem/Quine *network model* of theories and extending it, as Quine does in 'Two dogmas of empiricism' (1953), to language as a whole. The picture which Quine presents there is one of language as an articulated structure which makes contact with reality only at the periphery. Such a picture is intended to express the fact that the sentences of a language are related by various inferential connections, and that our understanding of any one sentence involves our apprehension of such connections. It is not necessary to discuss the ramifications of this view just now. I introduce it only as a way of making more vivid the point that even the least observational of sentences, i.e., those furthest from the periphery, are inferentially linked to others less far from the periphery.

We must also bear in mind a point touched on in Chapter 1: there is no evidence that a firm distinction can be drawn between theoretical and observational terms. A sentence is commonly described as "theoretical" because one or more of its terms are thought of as theoretical. But if no sense can be made of any firm distinction between theoretical and observational terms, then presumably none can be made of a firm distinction between theoretical and observational sentences. Quine, it is true, often talks of 'observation sentences', giving the impression that he thinks they constitute a distinct class, but elsewhere he recommends that one speak rather of 'observational sentences' or in terms of 'degrees of observationality'.[1]

What these remarks suggest is that the translator will have to attend closely to the various ways in which linguistic evidence can intersect with theoretical structure. Theory is underdetermined by evidence, but any body of sentences deserving to be called a theory has observational consequences and so has links with observational sentences. The formal structure of the truth theory requires a recursive generation of T-sentences across-the-board, from the relatively observational through the whole spectrum to the relatively non-observational. We can hope, then, that the overall pattern will give rise to the rich concept.

Another way of appreciating the various interrelations between the observational and the non-observational is by considering how a scientist's theory can be understood by his contempories, by which I mean not just those of the same "school", but rival theorists. Consider, for example, the origin of Dalton's theory of gases, an example I shall discuss at length in Chapter 5. Like any other theory, it did not suddenly appear, couched in a language quite removed from that of the rest of the physical science at the time. To put the matter in a rather Feyerabendian way, terms used in the theory had meanings partly determined by their links with other scientific terms in use at the time. Dalton talks, for example, of the 'atoms' or 'ultimate particles' of a gas as being those which are irreducible given the known techniques of 'chemical analysis and synthesis' (1808: 163).

---

[1] 1960: 42. Perhaps this is being too charitable to Quine. Christopher Boorse has argued that *all* of Quine's arguments for indeterminacy presuppose a clear observation/theoretical distinction (1975). If this is the case then Quine's doctrine is weakened to the extent that the distinction has been discredited.

Experiments are then described that involve these particles, and Dalton comments on the findings of Gay-Lussac and others in their work on gases. This made it possible for someone like Avogadro, who subsequently proposed what is commonly regarded as a rival, molecular theory of gases, to appreciate Dalton's ideas. Theoretical terms, in short, are constantly used in discussing experimental consequences and in the interpretation of previous work, and hence theories are intelligible to those besides their originators.

In talking of earlier scientific theories we are moving away from the field of radical translation or interpretation and coming closer to home, for our concern is not with present speakers of an alien language but with past speakers of a language very similar to our own. Such a move will mean that the translator will no longer be able to observe responses to verbal prompting, although qua interpreter his primary concern will still be with sentences held true and the principle of charity will still apply. This similarity might incline one to adopt a Quinean position to the effect that the only significant difference lies in the regulative maxims we are prepared to apply, but before discussing this let us first see if we can reach some tentative conclusion about how determinate interpretation will be if the programme I have outlined is carried out.

Since quantificational structure is presupposed in the alien language the radical interpreter will be able to overcome, as noted above, problems of logical form and inscrutability of reference (of the pervasive kind suggested by Quine's *gavagai* example anyway). Davidson is thus misguided in his reason for thinking there might still be indeterminacy at the level of predicates. Nevertheless, it is not clear from what he says that there will be *no* reason for thinking that there will be full determinacy at the predicate level. And despite the above remarks about the numerous interrelations of the theoretical and the observational, one might still feel that Quine has given, in his second objection, good reason for thinking there will. Although there cannot be two translations of a sentence, one, say, in subject-predicate form and the other not, we have as yet seen no conclusive reason for thinking there will not be many cases where an alien sentence s – 'remote from observationality' – may be translated by either of the home subject-predicate sentences p and q, even though p and q have different truth-values.

Ian Hacking has argued that such a situation could not arise in radical interpretation. The requirement of radical interpretation is that such statements of translation must match with T-sentences:

So there will be nothing to choose between a T-sentence 's is true if and only if p', provided in one system, and 's is true if and only if q', provided in another system. Yet we had the initial overriding requirement that T-sentences are true. Since p and q may be contraries, *both* T-sentences cannot be true. From Davidson's standpoint, this is a *reductio ad absurdum* of indeterminacy. (Hacking 1975: 154)

What Hacking overlooks, however, is the empirical nature of radical interpretation. Davidson emphasizes that the theory of truth for an alien language is tested by evidence that T-sentences are true (1973a: 321). Elsewhere he says:

If we treat T-sentences as verifiable, then a theory of truth shows how we can go from truth to something like meaning – enough like meaning so that if someone had a theory for a language verified only in the way I propose, he would be able to use that language in communication. (1973b: 84)

So on the basis of all the behavioural evidence we still might not be able to decide between incompatible theories of truth, and hence incompatible translation manuals, despite their being equivalent to each other in point of logical form.

Davidson's theory of radical interpretation might be thought of as an abstract reply to an abstruse doctrine. If Davidson is right, Quine's description of the methodological situation of the radical translator is inappropriate. Yet even if we agree that the radical interpreter is more faithful to our picture of one starting from scratch to understand an alien language, the claim that indeterminacy will be greatly reduced still looks somewhat speculative. What I propose to do now is to make some final points on this issue, concentrating on how it affects our interpretation of earlier scientific theories and suggesting that there is considerably more evidence available than has so far been mentioned.

Suppose we are trying to interpret Dalton's atomic theory of gases. The "primary" linguistic evidence we have available, let us imagine, consists of his published writings dealing with the theory, written communications with others, some laboratory notebooks, and discussions and interpretations of his work by others. From his own writings we manage to deduce a body of sentences asserted by him and hence, we assume, believed by him to be true. We begin to interpret these sentences, starting with the more observational, in such a way as to make Dalton consistent, and correct as often as possible. Since we have no difficulty in recognizing and translating the sentential connectives and quantificational devices, this proceeds quite smoothly, although we shall doubtless have to revise earlier translations and belief ascriptions as we go along. In particular, we must remember that we are guided by our own scientific lights here. Our present theories constitute our 'theory of nature' and so we must reckon them the standard by which we are to judge past theories.

If Quine is right in maintaining that there is no difference in principle between attempts to understand alien languages and attempts to understand other people in our own, then there will be definite limits to how far we can go in thus understanding Dalton:

Insofar as the truth of a physical theory is underdetermined by observables, the translation of the foreigner's physical theory is underdetermined by translation of his observation sentences. If our physical theory can vary though all possible observations be fixed, then our translation of his physical theory can vary though our translations of all possible observation reports on his part be fixed. (Quine 1970: 179–80)

The interrelations of the theoretical and the observational, and the comments I made about theory and observation with respect to interpreting previous scientific theories, suggest reasons for doubting this. In similar vein, attention might be drawn to the wide range of writings available as evidence. All of these will have their own situations, some involving connections with other scientific communities which will in turn be interrelated with larger linguistic communities. In particular, we can expect that in cases such as that of interpreting Dalton's theory there will be a chain stretching from a body of literature largely pertaining to one scientific community, through other bodies of literature centred on progressively more recent communities, reaching eventually to the writings of present-day scientists. Their various statements will in turn enjoy connections with the larger body of language which we ourselves share. We might call all of this "secondary" linguistic evidence. The more of it there is, the more it takes us away from the field of radical interpretation, but the more it emphasizes the point that in general any interpretation is based on a theory of truth for a language. It should not be surprising, therefore, if the evidence is vast.

Are there any other reasons for doubting Quine's claim? Another is forthcoming when we reflect on the fact that we think there are, at most, only a small number of things Dalton could possibly have been talking about. Given our knowledge of the state of physical science at the time, we can make empirically justified statements about what Dalton could have acquired knowledge of. We can form some idea, that is, of what he could have been causally acquainted with. This is where non-linguistic physical evidence, such as the scientific instruments Dalton used, is valuable to us, particularly when considered along with any laboratory notebooks and reports of experiments. From them we are able to realize, for example, that because his apparatus was not nearly sophisticated enough he certainly could not have confused things at the atomic level with things at the sub-atomic level. We are also able to establish (from interpreting observation reports alone!) exactly what techniques of chemical analysis and synthesis Dalton was familiar with. So if Dalton says, as he does, that 'atoms' were irreducible given the known techniques, we can even repeat his experiments in order to better understand what particles he was dealing with.

Here we are beginning to draw on some points that I shall present at length in the next two chapters when I talk about the causal account of reference and some actual cases of theory change. Apropos of some remarks about how to discover the referent of a proper name, I will propose a condition, analogous to the following one governing the use of a natural kind predicate within a linguistic community: for a natural kind predicate "φ" to be used by members of a linguistic community C to describe ψs, it is necessary that there be some causal connection between ψs and members of C, namely that between ψs and what is believed about what are called "φ"s in C. As it stands this is a somewhat rough-and-ready principle, but the idea behind it seems to hold good. For Dalton to have propounded a theory, and hence to have had beliefs, about what we call molecules, and what he called 'atoms', he must have been in a position to obtain causally knowledge of them through experiment. To take another case: for us to translate Mendel's '*bildungsfähig Element*' as "gene", it must be the case that genes were primarily responsible for the phenomena which he observed in his experiments on varieties of *Pisum sativum* and which he tried to interpret in his 1865 paper on plant hybridization.

This idea receives considerable support from the writings of Putnam and Kripke. In 'Explanation and reference', Putnam begins by arguing that what is important in discovering the extension of a physical magnitude term like "electric charge" is knowing that there should have been an 'introducing event' in which the term was correctly applied (1973: Section 2A). Such an event is one where there is a causal connection between the introducer of the term and what we recognize as an instance. By way of example, he asks the reader to imagine him standing next to Franklin as he performed his famous experiment with the kite. From this, he says, he is able to acquire the term "electricity", and consequently the term "electric charge". He then extends his argument to natural kind predicates:

For natural kind words too, then, linguistic competence is a matter of knowledge plus causal connection to introducing events (and ultimately to members of the natural kind itself). And this is so for the same reason as in the case of physical magnitude terms; namely, that the use of a natural kind word involves in many cases membership in a 'collective' which has contact with the natural kind, which knows of tests for membership in the natural kind, etc., only as a collective. (Putnam 1973: 205)

The causal account of how the extension of a predicate is established suggests an important constraint on discovering what earlier scientists were talking about, and hence on interpreting their theories. In the case of natural kind predicates it is clear how the causal network is secured, since such predicates apply to things in virtue of their physical properties. Despite Putnam's claims to the contrary, however, the causal account is not so obvious in the case of non-natural kind predicates like physical magnitude terms. Putnam's discussion and example seem to slide from the physical magnitude term "electric charge" to the natural kind predicate "flow of electric charge", and thence to "electricity". In Chapter 5 I shall consider physical magnitude terms at greater length.

When Putnam published 'Explanation and reference' in 1973, he was an advocate of a 'causal theory of reference', an expression the accuracy of which will be challenged in the following chapter. During the next five years he changed his mind and came to regard it as 'a theory of how reference is specified' (1978: 58), not of what reference is. With this new appellation we can well agree, for an important factor in discovering what the referent or extension of a term is, is how it came to be specified. As we have seen, this involves certain physical facts about the relation of the introducer or specifier to the world. But since there are such physical facts, one may wonder why it is that Quine excludes them in his purview of translation.

In the first section of this chapter, I cited Quine as explaining the difference between indeterminacy of translation and underdetermination of physical theory by evidence using these words:

Consider, from this realistic point of view, the totality of truths of nature, known and unknown, observable and unobservable, past and future. The point about indeterminacy of translation is that it withstands even all this truth, the whole truth about nature. This is what I mean by saying that, where indeterminacy of translation applies, there is no real question of right choice; there is no fact of the matter even to within the acknowledged underdetermination of a theory of nature. (Quine 1969c: 303)

The totality of physical facts, Quine is saying, fails to determine the correct translation. But there is a striking contrast between such talk about 'the whole truth of nature' and the restriction of this truth, in discussion of inscrutability and indeterminacy, to facts about behaviour. We agreed early on that theory is underdetermined by evidence and that the translation of observational sentences is determined by the behavioural facts. Suppose we were now to agree that the translation of observational sentences does not determine the translation of theoretical sentences. Even so, to get the required conclusion that the translation of theoretical sentences is not determined by the totality of physical facts, *Quine needs the additional premise that the only physical facts relevant to translation are behavioural.* But clearly the totality of behavioural facts forms only a small part of the totality of physical facts. So why is it that Quine thinks only the behavioural ones are relevant to translation?

We touched on what I think is the answer in Chapter 2. There we agreed to follow Quine in not requiring, in discussing inscrutability of reference, facts other than those which relate to the behaviour of language users. Quine begins the preface to *Word and Object* as follows:

Language is a social art. In acquiring it we have to depend entirely on intersubjectively available cues as to what to say and when. Hence there is no justification for collating linguistic meanings, unless in terms of men's dispositions to respond overtly to socially observable stimulations. An effect of recognizing this limitation is that the enterprise of translation is found to be involved in a certain systematic indeterminacy.

Ten years later he reaffirms the same point:

Meanings are, first and foremost, meanings of language. Language is a social art which we all acquire on the evidence solely of other people's overt behaviour under publicly recognizable circumstances. Meanings, therefore, those very models of mental entities, end up as grist for the behaviourist's mill. Dewey was explicit on the point: 'Meaning . . . is not a psychic existence; it is primarily a property of behaviour.' (Quine 1969a: 26–7)

In one sense, of course, Quine is right to say that we acquire language from our observations of other people's overt behaviour. But it seems obvious that although we *begin* to acquire language in this way, we can *progress* by relating these observations to the wider body of physical information we are able to obtain about them and the world. In like manner we develop a theory of, say, quasars not just from observing their behaviour but by relating it to a wider body of physical theory. Similarly, when it comes to translation our parameters are fixed by our 'theory of nature', by the totality of known physical facts, and these may outrun the behavioural ones.

This leads us back to the third stage of Quine's argument, to whether translation is indeterminate, as he says it is, or just underdetermined, as the rest of physical theory is. Dagfinn Føllesdal has claimed that the essential point for this stage, one that nobody who has discussed Quine's views appears to have fully understood, is that all the truths there are, are included in our theory of nature. He goes on, 'in our theory of nature we try to account for *all* our experiences. And the only entities we are justified in assuming are those that are appealed to in the simplest theory that accounts for all this evidence' (Føllesdal 1975: 32). If what I have said is right, then *some* of our experiences – think here of Putnam standing next to Franklin – are only to be fully explained by considering the physical facts *in addition to* the behavioural ones. Our 'theory of nature' is what it says it is, not a theory of *behaviour*! The conclusion must therefore be that translation, like the rest of physical theory, is underdetermined by evidence; it has so far not been shown to be indeterminate.

In this section I have maintained that there is no reason for thinking that Davidson's theory of radical interpretation will resolve all problems of determinacy, even given the diversity and complexity of the possible linguistic evidence. As for the constraint suggested by the causal account of how the extension of a predicate is specified, this only permits the scrutability of reference; it does not guarantee that we shall be able to capture the full sense of the term. Being able to discover what was causally responsible for the knowledge that Dalton, Mendel, Franklin, etc., had is not the same as being able to resolve all problems as to the meanings they attached to the terms they used. For we are relying on a theory of how extensions are specified, and this is quite different from a theory of how meanings are to be attributed. Even under the theory of radical interpretation, then, the path from reference to meaning is narrow at best and might sometimes peter out. So it seems we are obliged to hold that scrutability of reference does not imply that translation is determinate. Our choice of a theory of truth for a language might to this extent be underdetermined by the physical evidence.

This recalls an argument from Section 1 of the previous chapter. I said that if scrutability of reference did imply determinacy of translation, then indeterminacy of translation implies inscrutability of reference, in which case our being unable to translate determinately would preclude our assigning referents or extensions to alien terms. In this section we have seen that scrutability does not imply determinacy of translation. Simply because we are able to show that Dalton had a theory about molecules, it does not follow that we shall be able to establish the totality of his beliefs about them. Likewise, to return to the familiar example, merely because a radical *translator* can tell, by using the procedure outlined in Chapter 2, that members of an alien tribe are referring to rabbits and not rabbit stages, etc., when they use the term *"gavagai"*, it does not follow that he will thereby be able to interpret their whole "theory" of rabbits. It might be the case, for example, that they have beliefs of a religious kind about rabbits, beliefs which are not rendered determinate even within the theory of truth which the radical *interpreter* establishes.

Since scrutability does not imply determinacy, it cannot be said that failure to translate determinately implies inscrutability of reference. A theory of truth for a language might be underdetermined, but this does not in itself give us a reason for thinking that we cannot discover what particular names of the language refer to or what particular predicates of the language have as their extensions. On the other hand, of course, we have not established the much stronger conclusion that we shall *always* be able to discover this. We have to take each case separately and weigh the evidence. In doing so we are with Quine when he says 'knowledge, mind and meaning are part of the same world that they have to do with, and . . . they are to be studied in the same empirical spirit that animates natural science' (1969a: 26), though we might beg to differ over what those words mean.

4

Cluster theories of reference

1 NATURAL KIND PREDICATES AND PROPER NAMES

During the course of the last chapter we left off directly answering our four questions in order to examine an argument of Quine's which purports to show that there is no fact of the matter about intentional states such as belief. If Quine's argument were correct, and in addition the scrutability of reference were to imply the determinacy of translation, then it would also succeed in showing that the references or extensions of many of the terms used by alien speakers, and even by our ancestors, were inscrutable. By extending Davidson's theory of radical interpretation in accordance with the methodology of Chapter 2, and by drawing attention to certain non-behavioural constraints that may be imposed on interpretation, I concluded that Quine had shown neither that a realist approach to intentional states must be rejected nor that the lack of determinacy attaching to the interpretation of ancestral, or even alien, predicates rendered their extensions inscrutable. We can now go back to our task of answering the remaining three questions with the assurance that Quine has not given a decisive *a priori* argument against an epistemic, or intentional, theory of reference. Moreover, such a theory of interpretation is needed to provide the very evidence about belief on which this sort of theory of reference is based. According to my account, a realist theory of reference is in this way grounded in a theory of interpretation. Let us see how.

The central idea for the realist's account of the growth of scientific knowledge is that many subsequent theories give better descriptions of just those things which were the subjects of earlier theories. I have mentioned several examples which might plausibly be interpreted in this way: Dalton's atomic theory was superseded by Avogadro's; the Bohr–Rutherford theory of the electron by present-day theories; Muller's theory of genes by the theories of modern molecular biologists. The realist does not claim that every change of theory is of this kind, for sometimes, as in the cases of "phlogiston", "luminiferous ether", and "magnetic flux", we say that there is no one predicate now used which has the same extension as an earlier theoretical predicate. (One question we have yet to tackle is what makes these cases different.) What he says is that, by and large, scientists do, as a matter of fact, search for better theories about the kinds of things there are, and that science progresses because this methodology works.

The sorts of scientific predicates we are dealing with are often of a theoretical kind. To continue with the examples used in the previous paragraph, "atom", "gene" and "electron" might be so characterized. By contrast, some familiar predicates occurring in scientific theories might be thought of as observational, for example, "gold", "water", "quartz", and "mammal". These predicates can be correctly applied to objects of common experience. Correct application of theoretical predicates, on the other hand, depends on there being a certain amount of sophisticated apparatus. Water and gold are encountered in daily life in a sense in which genes and electrons are not. Also, correct application of predicates of an observational kind frequently requires little or no understanding of scientific theory.

There are other predicates, too, which are like observational scientific ones but which occur less frequently in scientific theories, predicates such as "lemon", "tiger", "oak tree", and so on. What these predicates have in common with predicates of the first two kinds, though, is that they are general names, characteristically associated with *natural kinds*. It is natural kind predicates that we are primarily concerned with.

There is no need for us to attempt to achieve a precise definition of what a natural kind is, but it is worth mentioning some features of them and of the predicates associated with them. To begin with, natural kind predicates do not usually admit of simple, precise definitions; as Putnam has said, they are 'cluster terms' (1962). "Oak tree" might be defined as "a member of the beech family with hard wood, jagged leaves, and which bears acorns", "gold" as "a yellow, non-rusting, malleable, ductile metal with atomic number 79". These may be contrasted with "bachelor", a general name not associated with a natural kind, which is commonly defined as "a man who has never been married". One interesting point which follows from this difference is that whereas "bachelor" cannot be correctly applied to an object that is either not a man or has been married, "oak tree" and "gold" can be applied to things that do not possess all the properties mentioned in their defining clusters; thus, many oak trees have leaves with smooth edges, and some gold is white. Putnam notes this point in saying that natural kind predicates are not synonymous with their definitions (1962: 53). We might identify something as belonging to a kind even though it does not possess all the properties characteristically associated with members of the kind. This idea of natural kind predicates being cluster terms will be of great importance when we come to give a theory of reference for them.

A common feature of natural kinds is that the properties used to define them are primarily physical. Oak trees and gold are recognized by the physical properties they exhibit. Bachelors, on the other hand, are not to be distinguished from other men by physical properties but by a "legal" property, viz., whether or not they have been married. Natural kinds are also commonly thought to be of explanatory importance and so become suitable subjects for scientific investigation. Consequently, many of the scientific predicates of interest to the realist, when he talks about scientific progress, are associated with natural kinds.

Having mentioned natural kinds, let me now dissociate myself from several of the things commonly said about them. In the first place, I would not wish to take any analogy between general names and proper names to the extent that a general name is held to refer to a kind of thing, i.e., to a supposed abstract entity, just as most proper names refer to particular things. There are electrons and sets of electrons, but not, in addition, a kind of thing "electron". In the second place, I do not wish to commit myself to the modish view of Kripke (1972a) and Putnam (1975a) that natural kinds have essential properties, i.e., properties which nothing can lack and still be of the kind. More recent work has suggested that there are serious difficulties involved in trying to make sense of such a notion of essence (Zemach 1976; Dummett 1973: appendix to Ch. 5). During the course of this chapter I shall suggest that we can make sense of a more restricted notion – that of "relevative" or "epistemic" essentialism – but this, as Kripke emphasizes, is not the sort of essentialism to which he is committed.

One last remark that needs to be made is that there is a set of terms whose members are frequently cited in discussions of the growth of science, but which are not associated with natural kinds: terms like "temperature", "mass", "length", "energy", and "electric charge".

In scientific theories they are typically used to express measurements. They may thus be construed as representing relations between objects, or events, and numbers on some scale, or as predicate-forming functors taking numbers in one argument place (Churchland 1979: 101–3). In the next chapter I shall consider how far the theory of reference developed in this chapter for natural kind predicates can be extended to include these terms.

Our primary concern in this chapter will be with answering the question:

(3) What conditions have to be satisfied by a natural kind predicate "φ" and an object a in order for "φ", as it is used within a linguistic community C, to be correctly applied to a?

An alternative way of putting this question would be, what is it for an object to belong to the extension of a natural kind predicate as that predicate is used within a linguistic community? One important point to notice about the question is that predicate extension is relativized to use of the predicate within a linguistic community. It is clear that some restriction involving use has to be placed on an inquiry into what it is for a certain predicate to have an extension. Even though one linguistic community may use many of the predicates that another community uses, it does not follow that they are thereby talking about the same things. A mundane example arises when we reflect on the fact that whales were once thought to belong not to the natural kind associated with the term "mammal" but to that associated with the term "fish". After reclassification, speakers still used the same terms, although their extensions had changed. Another example is suggested by the following passage: 'The name "electron" was introduced by G. Johnstone Stoney (1826–1911), in 1891, not of course as the name of these particles, but as the name of the fundamental unit of electricity, namely, the electric charge on a hydrogen ion in electrolysis' (Cajori 1962: 359).

Given that the inquiry is to be made relative to use, the question is, whose use? The obvious choices are: (a) use within a linguistic community; and (b) use by an individual speaker. I have chosen (a) because it is more germane to the enterprise of explaining how it is that subsequent theories can be about the same things. A scientific theory is something shared by a community, usually a community of scientists. Of course, this community is composed of individuals, many of whom know the theory. But often a speaker uses a scientific predicate, or even a relatively non-scientific natural kind term, without fully understanding it. This raises numerous problems for questions like (3) if use is taken as relative to an individual speaker; I will draw attention to some of them later. By choosing (a), I hope to avoid them.

Before continuing it is as well to resolve now one problem which (a) might be thought to raise, namely that of how a linguistic community is to be identified. Scientists share theories and may thereby be grouped into communities. Does it not then beg the question to identify the scientists sharing the theories by the scientific community to which they belong? More generally, how can we decide who shares a language without some independent purchase on the notion of a linguistic community? Fortunately there is a separate means of identifying those language users who belong to the same linguistic community. We touched on it briefly in the previous chapter. It is that the same theory of interpretation works for their statements. If different users employ the same predicates but accord them different extensions then this will be revealed by the T-sentences for their language and they will be reckoned members of a different linguistic community.

Returning to question (3) itself, in answering it I shall make use of some of the ideas put forward in recent work on proper names. That this should be possible becomes apparent when it is recognized that there is a parallel question for proper names:

(3') What conditions have to be satisfied by a proper name "a" and an object a in order for "a", as it is used within a linguistic community C, to denote a?

Or alternatively, what is it for an object to be the referent of a proper name as it is used within a linguistic community? I shall begin my investigation of question (3) by considering how we might answer (3').

The theory of Frege's that I briefly outlined in Chapter 1 suggests one approach to answering (3'). In order to explain how certain identity statements could be informative, Frege was led to distinguish between the sense and the reference of a proper name. "Sense" he took to be a cognitive notion, something which is known by users of the name and which can be passed on to others. In the case of proper names which occur in natural language, as opposed to proper names occuring in a perfect language, he thought that the sense may be different for different speakers (Frege 1892: 58, fn.), but for both these types of case the sense of a proper name would still be that by which the referent is determined. Dummett puts this point as follows:

What is important about Frege's theory is that a proper name, if it is to be considered as having a determinate sense, must have associated with it a specific criterion for recognising a given object as the referent of the name; the referent of the name, if any, is whatever object satisfies that criterion. (1973: 110)

Before we can frame an answer to question (3′) on the basis of this theory, we need to decide what the sense of a proper name is as that name is used within a linguistic community. Ought we to interpret it as the intersection of the senses associated with the name by the members of the community, as the union of those senses, or as something more complex? Of course, the answer to (3′) would be straightforward if we had phrased it in terms of an individual speaker's use of a name: "*a*" would denote *a* if and only if *a* were that object which uniquely satisfied the criterion for recognition associated with the sense attached to "*a*" by the speaker.

One point that has to be taken into account here is captured by Putnam in his 'principle of the division of linguistic labour', i.e., the principle that:

Every linguistic community . . . possesses at least some terms whose associated 'criteria' are known only to a subset of the speakers who acquire the terms, and whose use by the other speakers depends upon a structured cooperation between them and the speakers in the relevant subsets. (1975*a*: 228)

As regards proper names, an example where Putnam's point is made clear is in our use of the name "Einstein", where we intend to refer to the famous scientist who first formulated the special theory of relativity, and so on. Many of those who use the name with this intention may not associate with it a criterion of recognizing the man; at best they only have a partial grasp of the sense. Nevertheless, there are dictionaries, encyclopedias, and more knowledgeable people who could provide the requisite information, and the realization that such sources may be appealed to grounds the use of the name within the community. Thus it would be a mistake to identify "sense within a community" with "intersection of senses for members of the community".

Putnam's principle might be further extended if it is thought that the criteria associated with a name might not even be fully known to *any* of the speakers. It might be that certain beliefs and items of knowledge regarding the bearer of a name are preserved in manuscripts and historical documents such as birth registers without anyone being aware of their existence, and it could be said that these were constitutive of the sense of the expression as it is used within a community whose members had access to the manuscripts and documents. In such cases we would have to say that "sense within a community" was something more than "union of senses for members of the community". To allow for such a possibility, I shall henceforth understand "the sense of a proper name as that name is used within a linguistic community C" as being given by a complex set of descriptions which may be arrived at on the basis of what is believed within C. "What is believed within C" is, in turn, to be understood as including "what is known within C". Seen in this light, sense is a function of belief, and what is believed within a community may exceed what is believed by its members.

This stipulation means that some allowance will have to be made for inconsistencies within a community. If inconsistent descriptions are attributed to the bearer of a name, then clearly only one at most can be true of the bearer. Consequently, if the sense is to provide a criterion for determining the reference, only one of the descriptions can be reckoned part of the sense.

This theory which we have developed might seem somewhat removed from Frege's pristine view. Sense is to be thought of as a complex notion which cannot be assumed to be given by a simple definite description and might change over time. We have, however, preserved what was crucial to Frege's view: sense is a cognitive notion which, in the case of a proper name, provides a criterion for determining the referent.

We are now in a position to give a first answer to question (3'). It might be loosely termed "Fregean":

(3'F) A proper name "a", as it is used within a linguistic community C, denotes an object a if and only if a is that object which uniquely satisfies all of the descriptions which could be consistently attributed to the bearer of "a" on the basis of what is believed within C.

Both the theory of reference encapsulated in (3'F) and Frege's original theory are examples of what have come to be known as *descriptive* theories of reference for proper names. They appeal only to beliefs and items of knowledge in order to determine what a name refers to. Other descriptive theories have been proposed by Wittgenstein (1953: para. 79), Searle (1958), and Strawson (1954: 191–2). Like (3'F) they take the sense of a proper name to be given by a cluster of descriptions; unlike (3'F) they do not maintain that the referent has to satisfy *all* of the cluster. Rather, the object named is that which satisfies a suitable number of them. A suitable number need not be a majority; allowance can be made for attaching more importance to some than to others. Consider, for example, our use of the name "Archimedes". We believe a number of things to be true of Archimedes: that he discovered the principle named after him, that he lived most of his life in Syracuse, that he once leapt from his bath and ran naked through the streets shouting "Eureka!", that he invented a mechanical screw used for irrigation, and so on. Not all of these beliefs need be assumed to carry equal weight in determining who "Archimedes" refers to. We might well consider satisfaction of, say, the first and second beliefs to be of primary importance.

There is good reason to revise (3'F) in order to account for this view. If historical research should suggest, for example, that one *Anaximedes* really invented what we call the "Archimedean screw", then we would normally conclude that this is something *Archimedes* did not do. Sticking to the letter of (3'F), however, we would be forced to conclude, on the basis of this one piece of information, that there was no such person as Archimedes, and this seems most implausible. More generally, there seems to be no reason for holding that a person has to have done everything we attribute to them before they can be said to be referred to when we use their name. After all, we often concede that we have made a mistake in our description of a person, even when that description embodies the best knowledge available to us. This idea of a weighted cluster also marks a further analogy between proper names and natural kind predicates. Let us reformulate (3'F) so as to take account of it:

(3'C) A proper name "*a*", as it is used within a linguistic community C, denotes an object *a* if and only if *a* is that object which uniquely satisfies a suitable majority of the descriptions which could be consistently attributed to the bearer of "*a*" on the basis of what is believed within C.

Before considering whether (3'C) is touched by certain criticisms which have been made of descriptive theories in general, I want to discuss one *a priori* objection which might be made to (3'C) itself. It concerns the expression "unique". In so far as (3'C) lays down the condition that there must be at least one object which satisfies a suitable majority of certain descriptions, it seems to accord perfectly well with our intuitions. However, in so far as it lays down the condition that there must be *at most* one object, the theory might be thought to be unsatisfactory as there may be many maximal consistent sets of beliefs each determining a different referent, or with some determining a null referent. The general case of this would be where there is evidence of equal strength and importance within a community C for the statements "N is φ" and "N is ψ", where "φ" and "ψ" may be complex predicates, but that the object a_1 satisfies "φ" while the different object a_2 satisfies "ψ". It is further assumed that the situation does not arise because of a simple ambiguity in the name "N".

There are two points which I should like to make in reply to this criticism. The first is that it must be remembered that (3'C) is grounded in the theory of interpretation given in Chapter 3. It is on this theory that we rely in order to obtain our information about the belief states of members of C. Seen in this context, i.e., in the context of giving a theory of truth for the language of C, what the criticism amounts to is the claim that we have equally good evidence for the two T-sentences:

(i) "N is φ" is true if and only if a_1 is φ; and
(ii) "N is ψ" is true if and only if a_2 is ψ.

The theory of interpretation requires that we match truth with truth throughout the language. Given the enormous amount of information which will usually be available there has to be some doubt that this constraint will not be sufficient to decide the matter.

The second point is that (3'C) does not itself imply that, should such a case arise, the proper name N simply does not refer. To be sure, it throws no light on how to resolve the question of what it does refer to, but this is not to say that the theory may not be supplemented in some way. Later in this chapter I shall suggest how this might be done so as to assist with the identification of a referent in particular cases. A supplement of a different kind is suggested by the recent work of Field. In Chapter 2, I noted his claim that we should base our semantic theory on what he calls generalizations of the notions of denotation and signification, such as partial denotation and partial signification (Field 1973, 1974). I shall discuss his main example, Newton's use of the term "mass", in the next chapter. The gist of it is that we have equally good evidence for interpreting Newton's term "mass" as either of the special relativity terms "proper mass" and "relativistic mass". If Field's description of this example is correct then it may be thought of as very like an instance of the general situation hypothesized above. Field concludes that Newton's word "mass" *partially denoted* each of proper mass and relativistic mass (Field 1973: 476). Now an obvious, but apparently substantial, criticism of the suggestion that such a notion might replace that of denotation as part of the basis for semantic theory is that the first is conceptually parasitic on the second. That is, before we can understand what it is for a term to partially denote an object we have to understand what it is for a term to denote *sans phrase*. Our understanding of what it is for a term like "Archimedes" to denote is prior to our (comparatively sophisticated) understanding of what it is, or would be, for a term like "mass" to partially denote. This is not, however, a point which I shall pursue here. What I want to suggest is that we might wish to reject Field's claim that partial denotation is a more fundamental notion than denotation but retain it as a possible supplement to the theory contained in (3′C). In this way (3′C) would still define what it is for a proper name to denote, and it would also cater for those instances, should any arise, where (3′C) could not resolve two or more alternatives equally supported by the evidence available from interpretation.

Let us now see how (3′C) shares certain features with other descriptive theories. One important such feature is that the referent of a proper name is fixed by certain beliefs. In the case of "Archimedes", the referent, for a linguistic community C, is that person (if any) who satisfies a suitable majority of those descriptions which could be attributed to him on the basis of what is believed within C. If it should turn out that one Anaximedes is so identified then "Archimedes", as used within the community, denotes Anaximedes, despite the fact that there may have been some other person, contemporaneous with Anaximedes, who was named "Archimedes".

An illustration involving a case like this is afforded by the Gilbert and Sullivan operetta *H.M.S. Pinafore*. Towards the end, Buttercup, a nurse and child-minder, confesses that some years previously she mixed up two babies. One, Ralph, grew up to be an ordinary seaman, while the other, Corcoran, became captain of the Pinafore. According to a descriptive theory, it could be said after the confession that, in using the name "Corcoran", people before the confession thereby succeeded in referring to Ralph.

Another important feature of descriptive theories, at least as I have presented them, is that, since the sense or meaning of a proper name is given by the same set of descriptions used to fix the referent, it would be meaningless to deny that the referent satisfied those descriptions. If the sense of the name "Archimedes" is given by the four descriptive phrases mentioned above, then the statement "Archimedes did not discover the principle named after him, nor live most of his life in Syracuse, nor run naked through the streets shouting 'Eureka!', nor invent a mechanical water-screw" would be contradictory. Conversely, we can say that the statement that he did do a suitable majority of these things is necessarily true.

These and other consequences of descriptive theories have been subject to stringent criticism by Kripke in his paper 'Naming and necessity' (1972a). According to Kripke, it is a mistake to think that such theories either fix the reference of a proper name or give its meaning. He argues that what one must do, in order to understand which object is referred to by a name, is to look at how that name came to be used in the linguistic community. In the next section we shall consider his criticisms in detail. My main argument will be that what he succeeds in drawing attention to is a feature of the use of proper names which is relevant to the epistemological question "How can we discover what the referent of a proper name is as that name is used within a linguistic community?", but not to the conceptual question of what reference consists in. That is, he draws attention to a feature relevant to answering the proper name version of question (2) of Chapter 1, not question (3). Kripke has no *theory* of reference to offer, despite what others might claim. All he gives is an account of how we might decide, in certain cases where (3'C) proves inadequate, what is being referred to.

2 KRIPKE'S REMARKS ON NAMING

To be fair to Kripke, he does not explicitly mention the descriptive theory embodied in (3'C). His criticisms relate primarily to those theories in which the reference of a proper name is made relative to a speaker's use of the name. Against these he employs several examples, like the "Einstein" one given above, which appear to be conclusive (1972a: 292–3). Some of his criticisms, however, are more general, and it is clear that he thinks they are telling against any theory which implies that the referent of a proper name is whoever or whatever satisfies a certain set of descriptions.

One point which Kripke makes much of is that a proper name may be introduced via a definite description without its thereby coming to be held as synonymous with it (1972*a*: 274 ff.). There is no reason why this point cannot be accommodated by one who holds a cluster version of the descriptive theory, such as (3'C). In fact, recalling Putnam's point about cluster concepts, he would seem to be committed to it. The name "Mars" may have been introduced via the definite description "the red star", but as we learn more and more about the planet so the sense of the name changes.

Kripke then goes on to offer a general argument for why the sense of a proper name could never coincide with that of a definite description: names behave differently from definite descriptions in modal contexts. An extensive reply to this argument has been given by Dummett (1973: appendix to Ch. 5). Since proper names are being discussed in this chapter as something of a means to an end, it is not appropriate to involve ourselves in the details of what Dummett says. His main conclusion is that for modal contexts in general, there is no relevant difference between proper names and definite descriptions (1973: 131). The one qualification he adds is that this is not so when the name or the description is preceded by the verb "to be" or "to become". But the reason for this is said to be not a general feature of the behaviour of proper names in modal contexts; rather it has to do with the fact that a property like that of "being Archimedes" is not a property that can be acquired. Thus, the person who did most of those things attributed to Archimedes did not become Archimedes when he did them; he had always been Archimedes, because he had always been the one who in fact was to do most of those things. One might question here the propriety of speaking of Archimedes as "the one who was to do most of what is attributed to Archimedes". Is it not possible that Archimedes might not have done *any* of those things attributed to him? This is in fact another argument which Kripke uses to cast doubt on descriptive theories; we shall examine it shortly.

What is more relevant from the point of view of the analogy I have drawn between proper names and natural kind predicates, and my attempt to throw some light on what it is for a natural kind predicate to have an extension, is what Kripke says about how the reference of a proper name is fixed. Against the descriptive theorist's account of this, Kripke presents the following purported counter-example:

Imagine the following blatantly fictional situation . . . Suppose that Gödel was not in fact the author of [the incompleteness] theorem. A man named

'Schmidt', whose body was found in Vienna under mysterious circumstances many years ago, actually did the work in question. His friend Gödel somehow got hold of the manuscript and it was thereafter attributed to Gödel. On the view in question, then, . . . we, when we talk about 'Gödel', are in fact always referring to Schmidt. (1972a: 294)

Kripke thinks that such a conclusion is quite wrong, and he is right to think so. But he is mistaken if he thinks that a descriptive theorist must be committed to it. What makes a counterfactual situation like the one given intelligible is that the sense of the name "Gödel" is given by a cluster of descriptions which together provide a criterion for determining the referent. Schmidt would have had to have done more than to have first proved the incompleteness theorem in order for him to be the one to whom we refer when we use the name "Gödel". One might of course consider the case where the *only* thing that is believed about Gödel is that he was the first to prove the incompleteness theorem. Then a question would arise, given Kripke's fictional situation, as to whether users of the name had a false belief about Gödel or a true belief about Schmidt. Presumably, Kripke would take the former to be the case (1972a: 348 fn. 36). The problem with this view, however, is that it renders unanswerable the question "Who, then, is this Gödel about whom the users of the name had a false belief?". For obviously any answer, even "The man who was named 'Gödel'", would provide a criterion other than that associated with the original belief for recognizing the referent of the name "Gödel". In sum, Kripke's example is only telling against one who holds strictly to a Fregean theory like (3'F); it has no force against one who holds a cluster of descriptions theory like (3'C).

Perhaps the most important example which Kripke gives concerns the name "Aristotle". It is similar to the Gödel one in that Kripke considers it to be telling against the descriptive theorist's account of how the referent of a proper name is fixed. But it goes beyond the Gödel one in attempting to cast doubt on what the descriptive theorist thinks the sense of a proper name is. Here is the key passage:

Not only is it true *of* the man Aristotle that he might not have gone into pedagogy; it is also true that we use the term "Aristotle" in such a way that, in thinking of a counterfactual situation in which Aristotle didn't go into any of the fields and do any of the achievements we commonly attribute to him, still we would say that was a situation in which Aristotle did not do these things. (1972a: 279)

Despite Kripke's claims to the contrary, it would be wrong to construe this argument as one which calls into question the descriptive theorist's view that the referent of a proper name is fixed by certain beliefs. If we take the name "Aristotle" and successively deny the truth of the usual descriptions given of him, there soon comes a point where the natural reaction is to say "Who are you now talking about?". Thus, if someone says "Aristotle did not study with Plato, nor teach Alexander the Great, nor write the *Metaphysics*, nor . . .", one soon wonders whom is being referred to. The point at issue here is similar to that raised in our earlier discussion of McGinn's attempted refutation of Davidson. Just as we had to assume that an alien language user had a certain minimum of true beliefs about ψs before we could translate his "φ" by our "ψ", so there must be a certain minimum number of descriptions true of Aristotle before it makes any sense to talk of there being a person Aristotle who did not do various things.

In reply to this, it might be said that what Kripke really meant to draw attention to, regardless of what he actually said, is the modal statement "Aristotle might not have studied with Plato, nor taught Alexander the Great, nor written the *Metaphysics*, nor. . .". However, if this is understood as "Aristotle might not have studied with Plato, and Aristotle might not have taught Alexander the Great, and . . ." then, although quite intelligible, it does not support the thesis that the referent of "Aristotle" is not fixed by at least *some* set of descriptions. If, on the other hand, it is understood as "It might have been the case that (Aristotle did not study with Plato, nor teach Alexander the Great, nor . . .)", the embedded sentence is simply the one originally found to be puzzling.

Kripke's argument is more plausibly construed as an argument against the view that the meaning of a name is given by a certain set of descriptions. We noted in the last section that, given (3'C), it is necessarily true that the referent of a proper name satisfies a suitable majority of the descriptions associated with the name. From this it follows that there should come a point where a conjunctive assertion like "Aristotle did not study with Plato, nor teach Alexander the Great, nor . . ." not only invites a query but actually results in contradiction.

It is interesting to note here that Kripke himself provides an argument that could, in some instances, be used to bolster the descriptive theorist's case. For Kripke, as was noted in Section 1, also wants to hold that objects have essential properties, where an essential property of an object is one which it could not have failed to have (1972a: 276 and Lecture III). The examples he gives of such properties involve their origin and substance. He argues, for example, that it is necessarily true that a person has the parents they do. Hence, if it were known that, say, Aristotle's parents were X and Y, it would be contradictory to assert of Aristotle that his parents might not have been X and Y.

It does not follow from this of course that one who supports a descriptive theory need accept such properties as essential, nor, indeed, that they need be committed to any form of Kripkean essentialism. What does seem to be inescapable, however, is that some more or less complex description is necessarily true of whoever or whatever is the bearer of a proper name. Or at any rate this will be so unless it is maintained that a cluster of descriptions determines the referent of a name but does not give its meaning. One who holds this last position would seem in turn to be committed to denying that names have meaning. For it is difficult to see that anything could be made of the view that names do have meaning, that what fixes the referent of a name is a criterion associated with what is believed about the bearer, but that the meaning of a name is not given by what is believed about the bearer.

I shall not discuss in detail the position just mentioned which does not accord names meaning, for it marks a radical departure from the Fregean tradition. The meaning of a word, according to Frege, is just what a person knows when they know how to use the word, and so to deny that names have meaning seems to render unintelligible what a person's grasp of the use of a name consists in. If this criticism holds good, then one who wants to adopt a broadly Fregean view will have to hold that a cluster of descriptions not only fixes the referent of a name but also gives its meaning.

Returning to (3'C), we can say that one who wished to accept this account of how the sense or meaning of a proper name is to be specified would be committed to holding that it is necessarily true that the object which uniquely satisfies a suitable majority of the descriptions which could be consistently attributed to the bearer of a name on the basis of what is believed within a linguistic community C, does satisfy some subset of those descriptions. Such a consequence of holding a descriptive theory might at first seem unpalatable. What needs to be borne in mind, however, is that the complex description which is said to be necessarily true of the bearer of the name is dependent on what is known and believed within the linguistic community in which the name is used. There is no imputation of necessary properties in the sense which Kripke calls metaphysical and which underlies his form of essentialism; the kind of necessity is purely epistemological. The descriptive theorist is not in the position of holding that certain things will be true of the bearer of a name come what may, but only that they are true relative to what is known and believed within some linguistic community in which the name is used. In our own case, given those descriptions which we now believe to be true of Aristotle, it is not possible that a suitable majority of them should turn out not to be true of *Aristotle*. The suggestion that this might be so is tantamount to suggesting that the name "Aristotle" is being analysed as it is used within a different linguistic community from our own. The only sense which we can attach to the name, the only sense it has for us, depends on how we use it, and this is revealed by what we are prepared to believe about Aristotle. As we shall see in Section 3, this notion of "epistemic essentialism" can be made out for natural kind predicates too.

So far in this section we have looked only at Kripke's negative remarks about the theory of naming and not at his positive ones. I have argued that even though his arguments may have some force against certain descriptive theories, they have very little against the theory contained in (3'C). In particular, they certainly do not tell against (3'C) construed as a theory of how the referent of a proper name is to be determined. Kripke does have his own account of how the referent of a proper name is to be determined. Furthermore, although he denies that names have meaning or sense of the cognitive kind that we have been talking about, he does make use of a function which he sees as performing a similar role in some contexts. What we now have to do is to see whether these views add anything to the theory of (3'C) about what it is for a proper name to refer.

As I have emphasized already, our main concern is with understanding what determines the referent of a name, for we eventually want to cast light on how we can decide what natural kind predicates have as their extensions. I shall therefore have little to say about Kripke's notion of meaning. The picture he presents in 'Naming and necessity' is one in which the meaning of a singular or general term is a function from possible worlds to objects or sets of objects. Thus, the meaning of the proper name "Archimedes" is a partial function which assigns, to each possible world for which it is defined, the object which, in that possible world, is the referent of the name. The problem with this view is that although it might be technically useful in the semantics of modal logic, it in no way elucidates our understanding of what the meaning of a name is. Before we can check to see which object is assigned to "Archimedes" in world w_1, we shall have to decide whether or not w_1 is a possible world relative to this one. How are we to decide this? Evidently it will depend on what counts as a necessary truth, i.e., on what is stipulated as true in all possible worlds. But what this means is that we shall first have to decide such things as whether or not a particular attribution to "Archimedes" is possible, and the only way to do this is by reflecting on what meaning, in the cognitive sense of that term, the name "Archimedes" has. In order to decide whether or not "Archimedes" might have referred to some particular individual, we shall need to reflect on what can truly be said of Archimedes, and this presupposes that we already have an account of the descriptive, cognitive kind of what the meaning of the name is.

Turning to what Kripke says about how the referent of a name is to be determined, it must be noted that Kripke himself denies that he is giving necessary and sufficient conditions for when a name can be said to refer to a particular object. His causal account, unlike the descriptive theories of the last section, offers no way of eliminating the notion of reference. To see why, we need to have an outline of the causal account before us. As Kripke observes, it is difficult to state precisely, but for the purposes of discussion I shall assume as standard some such account as the following: there is a name-giving ceremony in which the object is named by ostension, or the referent fixed by a description. Subsequent speakers then intend to use the name to refer to the same object. In this way a causal network develops, and in order to determine what a name refers to, as it is used in some community of speakers, one has to trace back through the network to the original ceremony (see Kripke 1972a: 301–2).

The inclusion in this account of the condition that subsequent users of a name must intend to refer to the same object means that the notion of reference cannot be eliminated. The reason for including the condition is straightforward. To take an example of Kripke's, if I call my pet aardvark "Napoleon", this may be causally connected with the use of the name for the Emperor, but should lead to no identification of the Emperor with my aardvark.

Dummett has criticized Kripke's causal account on two grounds. The first is that it fails to explain what the required intention is an intention to do: 'Each speaker must intend to refer to the same object as the speaker from whom he heard the name: but what is it to refer to an object?' (Dummett 1973: 149). Evidently an answer to this question is required before we can explain what it is that a speaker must intend to do in order that his use of a name count as another link in the causal network. Descriptive theories provide answers to this question and so it would seem that they are theories of reference in a sense in which Kripke's causal account is not.

The second objection which Dummett raises is that it seems inevitable that there will be cases where the intention to preserve reference is fulfilled, but even so the referent is unwittingly transferred. In such cases it would not be possible, even in principle, to trace the causal network back in the way suggested by Kripke's account. An actual example where this appears to have happened is given in a paper by Gareth Evans (1975). He quotes from Isaac Taylor's book, *Names and their History*: 'In the case of "Madagascar" a hearsay report of Malay or Arab sailors misunderstood by Marco Polo . . . has had the effect of transferring a corrupt form of the name of a portion of the African mainland to the great African Island.' Such a situation is perfectly intelligible to us because we have a criterion, although imprecise, for "the same geographical area", and we have a criterion for determining what geographical area a place name is being used as the name of, independently of the actual origin of the name. A cluster theory like (3'C) explains what the latter criterion is. As Dummett remarks, however, Kripke's causal account 'leaves no room for the occurrence of a misunderstanding: since to speak of a misunderstanding would presuppose that the name did in fact have a sense which could be misunderstood' (1973: 150). Consequently, it is unable to make intelligible to us how it is that what is now a name for an island was once a name for a part of the mainland. Moreover, it also fails as an account of what the referent of a name is because a causal network of the kind envisaged does not guarantee that reference is preserved (but see Kripke 1972b).

Dummett draws this conclusion about Kripke's remarks on naming:

We are left with this: that a name refers to an object if there exists a chain of communication, stretching back to the introduction of the name as standing for that object, at each stage of which there was a *successful* intention to preserve its reference. This proposition is indisputably true; but hardly illuminating. (1973: 151)

But even if there is no causal *theory* of meaning or reference, it does not follow that Kripke has not succeeded in drawing attention to one feature of what it is for a name to refer that is an essential element of any acceptable theory. Ought we then to revise (3′C) to take account of this causal element? The case for the affirmative is well summed up by Evans:

There is something absurd in supposing that the intended referent of some perfectly ordinary use of a name by a speaker could be some item utterly isolated (causally) from the user's community and culture simply in virtue of the fact that it fits better than anything else the cluster of descriptions he associates with the name. (1975: 197)

At first this argument does seem to carry some weight. In the context of a theory like (3′C), the sort of situation which Evans has in mind would be something like the following: there is a linguistic community C in which a certain cluster of descriptions is associated with the name "N". Suppose that the object which best satisfies the cluster is a_1, but that a_1 is causally isolated from C and that some other object (or objects) is (are) causally responsible for those beliefs underlying the cluster. Which object is denoted by "N"? The answer suggested by (3′C) is a_1: although members of C might intend to refer to another object, they always succeed in referring to that object which best fits what is believed about the referent of "N" in C.

On further reflection, however, it can be shown that the point which this argument attempts to make is already encompassed by (3′C). The difficulty with the supposed situation, construed as an objection to a cluster theory, is in understanding how the object which best satisfies a cluster of descriptions could fail to be the one which is causally responsible for those beliefs underlying the cluster. Returning to the "Archimedes" example, how could it be that a person who satisfied a suitable majority of the descriptions "discovered the Archimedean principle, lived most of his life in Syracuse, ran through the streets shouting 'Eureka!', and invented the Archimidean water-screw" might turn out to be causally isolated from those very deeds which are described in the cluster? The situation is palpably unreal, and this marks something of importance about descriptive theories. What a name refers to depends on what is known and believed about the bearer of the name, but beliefs and items of knowledge themselves have a causal origin. As Evans says, 'the important causal relation lies between [the denoted] item's states and doings and the speaker's body of information – not between the item's being dubbed with a name and the speaker's contemporary use of it' (1975: 197). But explicit recognition of this causal relation is not something that has to be added to descriptive theories, it is already contained in them. Hence, the descriptive theorist's understanding of what it is for a proper name to refer to an object does not require supplementation of this kind.

Despite the criticisms brought against the causal account, it must be admitted that there are situations in which we can imagine causal origin playing an important part in discovering what the referent of a name is. These are where there is some dispute over who or what is being talked about. Some of them might be resolved by making use of the causal relation which Kripke emphasizes. Consider, for example, the following case. Erigena was a ninth-century philosopher also known as John the Scot. The little that is known about him may have been true of various people, each of them having done some of the deeds attributed to Erigena. What would seem to count as a crucial factor in deciding Erigena's identity, however, would be the discovery that one of those regarded as possible bearers of the name had in fact been named "Erigena". The causal relation between the introduction of a name and later use of it is of some importance when those descriptions associated with the later use turn out not to be uniquely true of something. In such cases the later users would presumably accept, as having particular relevance to the decision of the issue, evidence as to which of the various possible bearers of the name was so christened. This fact is readily accounted for by a cluster theory: one of the cluster of descriptions believed by users of the name "N" to be true of a_1, if a_1 is to be counted as the bearer of the name, is "was christened 'N'". Which is not to say, of course, that being christened with a name is necessary in order for something to count as the referent of the name; like each of the rest of the descriptions in the cluster, it is defeasible.

What lies behind this example is the point that, for a name to be successfully introduced into a language as the name of some object, there has to be a causal relation between that object and those who introduce the name. The object might not be present at the time, but in that case the object must be causally responsible for those beliefs underlying the descriptions which are associated with the object and which are therefore used to fix the referent of the name. As regards this latter type of case, numerous instances can be imagined where the causal origin of information is of particular relevance in discovering who or what is being referred to. By way of illustration, suppose that a manuscript is found which details certain events that took place in a monastery near Florence during the twelfth century. One entry, from around 1130, refers to a visiting philosopher and theologian, but it is not clear from the script whether it was Peter Abelard or Peter Lombard. Unfortunately the remarks made concerning this person are insufficient for us to decide which of the Peters it was. Upon further investigation, however, it is revealed that at the time the entry was written Peter Lombard was studying in nearby Bologna, whereas Peter Abelard was lecturing in Paris. It would therefore seem that the latter could not have been the one whom the author of the manuscript was referring to.

In general we can say that, in those cases where there is disagreement over who or what the referent of a proper name is, one factor which may resolve the disagreement is which of the possible bearers of the name, i.e., which of those objects satisfying a suitable majority of the descriptions associated with the name, the users of the name could have been causally related to. The point might be expressed in terms of a condition analogous to that mentioned in the previous chapter for natural kind predicates: for a proper name "a" to be used by members of a linguistic community C to refer to a, it is necessary that there be some causal connection between a and members of C, namely that between a and what is believed about the bearer of "a" in C. It is simply not possible that the members of C should be talking about something causally isolated from them. For this reason the condition might also be seen as an *a priori* constraint on possible attributions of referents to names.

What these remarks go to show is that although various features pertaining to what might loosely be termed the causal account of naming do not add anything to the cluster theory of naming, they are of some importance when it comes to discovering what a particular name refers to. That is, they are pertinent not to answering question (3'), but to answering the proper name version of question (2), the question:

(2') How can we discover what the referent of a proper name is as that name is used within a linguistic community?

What (3'C) suggests by way of answer to this question is that we must consider those beliefs associated with the bearer of the name within the community. We can now add that where such a method does not enable us to decide which of several objects is the referent, the causal relations between those objects and the community can sometimes decide the issue. Also, it can be said that satisfaction of the causal constraint noted above is a necessary condition for an object's being counted the referent of a name. In the next section I shall argue that these same remarks hold when we consider natural kind predicates instead of proper names.

3 A THEORY OF REFERENCE FOR NATURAL KIND PREDICATES

Question (3) is about natural kind predicates. In Section 1 of this chapter I explained how natural kind predicates could be thought of as cluster terms. I then pointed out that there was an analogous question to (3) which concerned proper names, and that proper names could also be thought of as cluster terms. In both the remainder of that section and Section 2 I discussed how this analogous question might be answered. The result was the cluster theory $(3'C)$. If this theory does provide an adequate answer to the question of what it is for a name to refer – and we have not seen any reason for seriously doubting that it does – then it would seem that a theory just like it should answer the question of what it is for a natural kind predicate to have an extension. My proposal, then, for an answer to question (3) is

(3A) A natural kind predicate "φ", as it is used within a linguistic community C, can be correctly applied to an object a if and only if a satisfies a suitable majority of those descriptions which could be consistently attributed to φs on the basis of what is believed within C.

Let me begin discussion of (3A) by noting that it does account for that aspect of natural kind predicates that leads us to call them cluster terms. By specifying that only a suitable majority of descriptions have to be true of an object in order for a natural kind predicate to be correctly applied to it, it is explicitly allowed that the object might not have all the properties associated with the kind. As for what counts as a "suitable majority", this is not something that can always be specified in advance. As a matter of fact, the question does not often arise. Just as in the case of a proper name where I argued that it would be rare to find more than one object which satisfies a large number of the descriptions associated with the name, so too with natural kind predicates it is not often that an object satisfies only enough of those descriptions associated with the predicate that it counts as what we might call a borderline case. The obvious exceptions are where the predicate is vague. The problem of how such predicates are to be dealt with semantically has been extensively discussed in recent philosophy of language. There are two main opposing views. On the one hand there are those like Dummett (1975) and Wright (1975) who, taking their lead from Frege, contend that vagueness invests our language with a basic incoherence and that therefore attempts to construct a logic capable of handling vague expressions are ill conceived. Central to their argument is the sort of example which leads to what is now generally referred to as the Sorites type of paradox. Suppose we have a heap of sand; the subtraction of one grain from the heap cannot make a relevant difference, so if $n + 1$ grains of sand constitute a heap so do n grains; eventually our "heap" seems to be winnowed down from many grains to none. How can we, then, specify a criterion of what it is for "heap" to have an extension? The position this gives rise to becomes particularly important if considered along with the claim that many scientific terms are ineluctably vague (Swinburne 1969), for this would imply a severe constraint on any attempt to give a comprehensive logic for scientific theories. On the other hand there are those who reject the Fregean view and have constructed many-valued logics for vague expressions (Zadeh 1975) or logics based on the semantic technique which has come to be known as supervaluation (Fine 1975). This last alternative has the attraction that it would justify the retention of all the laws of classical logic (Fine 1975: Section 4). Since, however, my concern with the theory of reference is primarily to explicate a realist account of scientific progress, I shall not pursue this problem further.

The idea of an object's satisfying a suitable majority of descriptions associated with a predicate is of particular use when it comes to explaining the growth of scientific knowledge. It allows for earlier scientists being partly wrong in what they said about members of natural kinds. At the end of the previous section I indicated how (3'C) provides the basis for an answer to question (2'): we discover what a name refers to as it is used within some community by looking at what is believed in that community about whoever or whatever is the bearer of the name. (3A) likewise provides the basis for an answer to question (2): we discover what a natural kind predicate has for its extension as it is used within some community by looking at what is believed in that community about things of that kind. By not making satisfaction of every description in the cluster necessary, our investigation of what members of a previous scientific community were talking about when they used a particular natural kind term in a theory can take into account the possibility that they had some mistaken ideas about things of that kind. This point might be expressed more generally by saying that (3A) shows how a natural kind predicate might not be strictly true of anything but still have an extension.

Herein lies the core of my answer to the sort of problem that prompted, in Section 2 of Chapter 1, the four questions. There I cited some examples of where our natural inclination is to say that earlier scientists were mistaken in their theories: Bohr thought that particles have simultaneous position and momentum, Muller believed genes to be composed of proteins. In fact there are countless other examples of this, both for communities of scientists and for users of natural kind predicates generally: Ptolemy maintained that the planets revolved around the earth, Dalton thought all molecules were monatomic, whales were once thought to be fish, Mendeleyev believed that chemical elements were fundamental and irreducible, according to Aristotle the brain's function is to regulate the temperature of the body, Maxwell held that light waves must be propagated through a material ether, and so on. These descriptions themselves incline us to say that Bohr was referring to atomic particles, Muller to genes, Ptolemy to the planets, etc. The theory (3A) provides the basis of a justification for using such descriptions.

It is, however, only the core of my answer. From the previous chapter we recall that, in deciding which beliefs were held by our ancestors, we are able to make use of a considerable amount of non-behavioural evidence and in this way supplement the elementary provisions of Davidson's theory of interpretation. In particular, just as there is a general *a priori* constraint on possible attributions of referents to singular terms, so there will be one on possible attributions of extensions to predicates: members of the linguistic community under consideration must have been in an appropriate causal relation to things of whatever kind we decide they were applying a predicate to. These points will be further clarified in the next chapter when we consider some actual cases of theory change. First we need to see exactly how (3A) answers question (3).

As was shown to be the case with the theory of proper names (3'C), (3A) is a theory both of how the extension of a natural kind predicate is fixed and of what the sense of a natural kind predicate is. They are both functions of what is consistently believed within the community in which the natural kind predicate is used. Within the linguistic community of modern physicists, for example, the term "electron" has as its extension just those things which satisfy a suitable majority of what they now believe to be true of electrons. Future physicists may dispute whether some of these beliefs are true of electrons; they might even accord the beliefs different weights and so arrive at a different "suitable majority"; but none of this would jeopardize the claim they may wish to make that they have developed a better theory of *electrons*.

The sense of a natural kind predicate is given by those descriptions which are associated with the predicate as it is used within a community. As with a proper name, this sense is not to be thought of as given by those descriptions which some member of the community associates with the term. Sense is cognitive and hence communicable, but of course a member of a community may not fully understand a term, and what this means is that he has only a partial, perhaps imperfect, grasp of its sense.

This situation becomes more complex with terms like "gold" which are used in everyday speech but also have a use in more technical contexts. Most of us, most of the time, successfully use the term "gold", but we would not be able to distinguish between a gold ring and a carefully prepared alloy one which contained no gold. As Putnam has pointed out, it would be absurd to say, in the light of this, that most of us just do not know what the meaning of the term is (1974: 449). We need not conclude from the example, however, as Putnam does, that the extension of the term "gold" does not depend on what is known, and therefore believed, about gold. We might follow Dummett in holding that we do fully understand the term even though we have not fully grasped its sense (1974: 530–1). One consequence of this view is that, if the meaning of a term is just what a person knows when they understand the term fully, then a wedge is driven between sense and meaning, for as Dummett concludes: 'The meaning of the word "gold", as a word of the English language, is fully conveyed neither by a description of the criteria employed by the experts nor by a description of those used by ordinary speakers; it involves both, and a grasp of the relationship between them' (1974:

531). To avoid this consequence we might stick to the simpler view that an ordinary speaker, because he has not fully grasped the sense of the term "gold", does not fully understand it and so only knows a part of its meaning. On neither alternative, however, is one forced to give up the view that the extension of a natural kind term depends on its sense, and that sense has to do with knowledge; the only difference is that, according to Dummett, part of this knowledge consists in grasping how everyday uses of a term like "gold" are related to its more technical uses.

Other examples designed to cast doubt on the cluster theory's account of the senses of natural kind predicates are offered by both Kripke and Putnam. Having noted how definitions of natural kind words mention clusters of properties, Kripke attempts to show that possession of most of these properties need be neither a necessary nor a sufficient condition for membership in the kind (1972a: 318). Despite the way Kripke phrases his claim, it is clear that he intends his examples to be conclusive against any form of descriptive theory, irrespective of whether it is in terms of most properties or a suitable majority of properties. What they would have to show, then, to be conclusive against (3A) is that given how, say, the natural kind term "tiger" is used within a particular linguistic community, it might turn out both that tigers should fail to possess a suitable majority of those descriptions consistently associated with them within the community, and that something could satisfy a suitable majority and yet not be a tiger.

Kripke's purported counter-example to the sufficiency condition requires us to imagine an animal being discovered which had all the external properties mentioned in the cluster associated with the word "tiger", but a completely different internal structure. Of course, Kripke is quite right to say that we would not count such an animal as a tiger. But as it stands, this example does not even begin to cast doubt on a cluster theory phrased in terms of a *suitable majority* of descriptions. Ordinarily we identify tigers by means of properties relating to external appearance, like "having four legs and a tawny yellow coat with transverse black stripes". But this is not to say that we accept these properties as definitive of the species "tiger", or that, if it came to precise definition, we should attach more weight to them than to properties relating to internal structure. Moreover, if, say, "reptilean tigers" started appearing, properties which enabled us to identify "mammalian tigers" would no doubt gain in importance.

The case which has to be argued in order to controvert the sufficiency condition of the cluster theory I have developed would be that an object could have a suitable majority of those properties attributable to φs on the basis of what is believed within a linguistic community C, and yet not be something to which the predicate "φ", given how it is used within C, could be correctly applied. In revising Kripke's tiger example, what would have to be maintained is that something could have all the properties that, for example, contemporary zoologists (the experts to whom we defer) accept as definitive of membership of the species, and yet not be a tiger. It is difficult to see that any sense can be made of such a suggestion. There might come a time when, as a result of further zoological investigation, the species is defined differently; this happened with whales. Similarly, the properties now regarded as definitives were not so regarded by earlier zoologists. But in these cases we are no longer considering the use of the natural kind predicate "tiger" within our own linguistic community.

The situation here is just like one we encountered in connection with proper names. The referent of the name "Archimedes", as that name is used within a community C, is that person who satisfies a suitable majority of those descriptions believed by members of C to be true of Archimedes, even if it should later turn out, as a result of subsequent investigation, that one Anaximedes is so identified. Later use of both names would no doubt reflect this discovery, with a resultant change in sense of the names. But in so far as we are considering whom members of C succeeded in referring to when they used the name "Archimedes", we must say it was Anaximedes.

Dummett has suggested a way of strengthening Kripke's example:

Suppose that there are on Mars creatures exactly like tigers, both superficially and in respect of internal structure. Then I think that they would still not be tigers (though doubtless they would be called 'Martian tigers'), because they would not be sprung from the same stock as real tigers, i.e., Earth tigers. A difference of internal structure serves to show that a creature is not a tiger by showing that it does not share a common descent with real tigers. For the same reason white ants are not really ants. It is a part of the meaning of a word like 'tiger' or 'ant' that it applies to an animal in virtue of its membership in a breed or family ('species' is of course too specific a term), i.e., a group connected by descent. (1974: 532)

Perhaps this version gains initial plausibility because the environment on Mars is so different from that on Earth; we cannot help thinking that any animal or plant found there must be of a quite different kind from any found here. If we make allowance for this, it becomes less convincing. Despite Dummett's parenthetical remark, the applicability of words like "tiger" and "ant" does ultimately depend on our concept of a species, rather than on the somewhat Biblical notion of 'sprung from the same stock'. Now "species" is a term like "acid" in that it has a common use as well as a more specialized one. We sometimes use it to refer to a group of individuals which share a distinctive, common property, thus following its usage by seventeenth- and eighteenth-century zoologists and biologists. In modern biological science, however, a specimen is usually counted a member of some species only if apart from distinctive physical properties it can also be mated or interbred with recognized members of the species to produce fertile offspring. This is the reason why white ants are not really ants, for although they might resemble them superficially they cannot form a breeding colony with them. The crucial test for whether or not an animal found on Mars was a tiger, i.e., a member of the species *Felis tigris*, would therefore be whether or not it could mate with tigers here on Earth to produce fertile offspring. If Dummett's description of the alien creatures is strictly adhered to, then it would seem certain that they could, and this would provide overwhelming evidence in favour of the conclusion that there were tigers on Mars. (Their presence there would then, for a time anyway, be a scientific anomaly.) If, on the other hand, the creatures did not mate with Earth tigers, then this would be taken as indicative of a physical difference which would tell against their being classed as members of the species *Felis tigris*.

All of this, however, takes us far beyond what Kripke has to say. His argument against possession of a suitable majority of properties being necessary for membership of a natural kind is even more sketchy than his argument against its being sufficient. He suggests it might turn out that, as a result of optical illusions or other errors, tigers actually have none of those properties characteristically associated with them. Now of course some things might not possess such properties, and in fact most things do not possess them – only tigers do; but how could it possibly turn out that *tigers* might not possess them? The point to be made here is analogous to the one made in the previous section against Kripke's claim that Aristotle might not have done any of those things commonly attributed to him. It is tigers we are considering, and tigers just are those things which characteristically have four legs, a tawny yellow coat, and so on. The only sense which we can attach to the term "tiger" – the only sense it has for us – depends on how we use it, and this reveals what we believe about tigers.

Putnam's purported counter-examples to cluster theories are more elaborate. As in the case of the "gold" example already mentioned, Putnam's aim is to show that one cannot hold both that 'the meaning of a speaker's words does not extend beyond what he knows and believes', and that 'meaning determines extension' (1974: 447). Accepting (3A) does not commit one to accepting the first of these theses; in fact, the reason we rejected it was precisely to take account of what Putnam calls the 'principle of the division of linguistic labour'. Consequently, we need not look at Putnam's elm/beech and aluminium/molybdenum examples since he adduces them in support of his principle and against the thesis (1974: 450).

Putnam's other reason for rejecting the conjunction of both theses has to do with what he calls 'the contribution of the environment' to determining the extension of the terms we use. The example he presents as an illustration of this would, if Putnam's interpretation of it were correct, tell against a cluster theory like (3A). It goes like this: suppose that, on a distant planet very similar to ours called "Twin-Earth", the colourless, tasteless liquid that comes down in rain, fills the oceans and lakes, etc., is not composed of H_2O molecules but of XYZ molecules. Furthermore, the Twin-Earthians use the term "water" to refer to the said substance. Suppose also that we are back in 1750 and, because chemistry is underdeveloped, neither Earthians nor Twin-Earthians know the chemical structure of what they respectively call water. Thus, an Earthian and his identical twin on Twin-Earth can associate exactly the same beliefs and items of knowledge with the term "water" and its extension. Yet, says Putnam, the extension of "water" as used by Earthians is H_2O, whereas its extension as used by Twin-Earthians is XYZ. This suggests a dilemma, either horn of which seems to lead to Putnam's desired conclusion. If we say that, because Earthians and Twin-Earthians know and believe the same things about water, "water" means the same for both, then, since the extension is different on the different planets, there must be something more to determining extension than looking at what is known and believed. If, on the other hand, we say that because the extension is different on the different planets "water" means something different, then this difference has to be explained in terms other than those which rely solely on what is known and believed. Therefore, either meaning does not, by itself, determine extension, or the meaning of a word extends beyond what is known and believed about what it can be correctly applied to (Putnam 1974: 451).

Obviously the crucial question to be asked about the example is whether Putnam is justified in assuming that the extension of the term "water" is different on the two planets. We can admit that *after* Earthians and Twin-Earthians have become chemically sophisticated the term will have a different extension. But then, with the help of the principle of the division of linguistic labour, it is clear that we could describe the situation as one in which the meaning of the term will be different on the two planets. Before such enlightenment, however, Earthians and Twin-Earthians would agree, *ex hypothesi*, in their every application of the term "water". So it would seem incumbent upon us to conclude that when nobody knew what the chemical nature of the stuff called "water" was, the extension of the term was the same on both planets. Once again we are reminded of the fact that the extension a term has is relative to its use within a given linguistic community.

Attention has been drawn by Zemach to an actual case very much like the one Putnam hypothesizes: the discovery of isotopes of water (1976: 120). Given the various forms of hydrogen and oxygen, together with their various combinations, it seems that we can now say that there are eighteen different kinds of water. Another actual case would be the discovery that chlorine has two common isotopes. These cases differ from Putnam's because the chlorine isotopes, and some of the water isotopes, occur together naturally and are not divided between planets. As a result it seems that, since it always was correct to apply the natural kind terms "water" and "chlorine" to samples containing the different kinds before isotopes were discovered, it always will be correct so to apply them.

Such examples are not likely to cut much ice (of any kind!) with Putnam. According to him natural kind predicates like "water" – supposing it to be one – are 'indexical', i.e., their extension is determined in virtue of some equivalence relation which makes use of an indexical word. In the case of "water", Putnam suggests 'the "same liquid" relation to *our* water' (1974: 451). This relation is, he says, a theoretical one whose discovery is to be made through scientific investigation of whatever it is that we now identify as water. Where the natural kind predicate is a substance term the relation will typically be a structural one: chemical formula in the case of "water", atomic number in the case of "gold".

This notion of indexicality is one which Putnam is keen to link with Kripke's notion of a 'rigid designator' (Kripke 1972*a*). Kripke accepts that both proper names and natural kind predicates are rigid designators: names designate the same thing, and natural kind predicates the same kind of thing, in different possible worlds. As was noted in the previous section, Kripke fills out the idea of sameness in terms of a thing's origin and structure; people could not have failed to have the parents they do, and elements could not have failed to have the atomic numbers they do. Putnam's view about "water" – the one he thinks his Twin-Earth example supports – is a short step away: water is whatever has the same chemical formula, given the present state of our chemical knowledge, as the substance we identify as water.

Returning to the isotopes, I think that even if they had been discovered on another planet and not on Earth, Putnam would dispute that they were analogous cases to his Twin-Earth one. The crucial question is: which properties are the essential ones? If "having atomic weight x" is one, then "water" and "chlorine" are not natural kind predicates, for they can be correctly applied to substances with different atomic weights. But such a conclusion goes against our ordinary usage of the terms. Even chemists, when they use the terms, use them in such a way that they can be correctly applied to separate instances, all of which share a large number of important properties. Furthermore, "having atomic weight x" seems not to be an essential property according to Kripke's favoured test for essentiality. "Could something be chlorine and not have atomic weight 35?". Apparently so; quite a lot of chlorine has atomic weight 37. And what this means is that a specimen of chlorine can pass all of the chemical tests for being chlorine and yet have a different atomic weight from another specimen which has also passed all of the tests. It would seem, then, that "having atomic weight x" is not a property regarded as essential relative to our system of chemistry, for the chemical properties of a substance are not directly related to its atomic weight.

When we look at the properties "having the chemical formula y" and "having atomic *number* z", the picture is different. It does seem that we would now say "Something could not be water (chlorine, gold) and not have the chemical formula (atomic number) H_2O (17, 79)''. According to our system of chemistry, these properties do seem to be essential. What this shows, however, is not that such statements are, in Kripke's phrase, 'necessary truths in the strictest possible sense' (1972*a*: 320), but that they are necessary relative to our system of chemistry or, more broadly, to our way of looking at the world.

Zemach points out that there have been radical changes in what science considers to be of the essence of things (1976: 121–2). The very presentation which Putnam gives of his Twin-Earth example goes to support this view. Despite the quotation just given, Kripke too seems to realize this: 'Any world in which we imagine a substance which does not have these properties is a world in which we imagine a substance which is not gold, *provided these properties form the basis of what substance is*' (1972*a*: 320; my emphasis). If we gave up atomic theory, perhaps in favour of sub-atomic theory or of some non-corpuscular theory, then no doubt "having atomic number x" would cease to be of central importance. Likewise, before 1750 there was nothing like the modern notion of an element, and so nothing *could* be said for distinguishing substances according to chemical formula. Hence the terms "water", "gold" and "chlorine" did not, before the introduction of the theories and techniques of chemical analysis, have meanings which determined the course to be followed. Once this is realized, Putnam's Twin-Earth example, far from showing that theses like the two he begins by distinguishing cannot be held, actually goes to support them!

Returning to Dummett's examples concerning the terms "tiger" and "ant", we can make a similar remark about membership of a species. The current state of the biological sciences suggests that fertile interbreeding is an essential property of a member of a species, i.e., that it is necessary that an animal or plant, if it is to be correctly described as belonging to a species "S", is able to interbreed or mate with recognized members of "S" so as to produce fertile offspring. But if we gave up the Darwinian tradition, or maybe just augmented it with a strong Lamarckian component, then this property may no longer be regarded as essential. Our understanding of what a species is may change, and with it the meaning of the term "species". One difference between species terms and substance terms, though, is that we seem far more reluctant to deny that an infertile animal or plant is a member of a species than we do to deny that a specimen of some substance with an unusual structure is a substance of the usual kind. Perhaps this marks a difference between the biological and the physical sciences.

However matters stand with these "relatively essential", or "epistemologically essential", properties, accepting that there are such does not imply that there is a rival theory of reference to (3A) or that (3A) is in some way incomplete. (3A) explicitly accounts for Putnam's observations about the importance of scientific theory in fixing the extensions of natural kind predicates by dealing with suitable majorities of properties and with what is believed within the community in which a predicate is used. "Suitable" allows us to attach more weight to some descriptions, and these might well be those suggested by the theories scientists accept. More generally, all of those descriptions which can be associated with a natural kind predicate, and hence those – if any – regarded as mentioning essential properties, will eventually be decided on the basis of what is believed within a community.

The indexical element of natural kind predicates that Putnam's theory attempts to characterize means that the essential properties are those of what is identified within a community as belonging to the kind. Because of this use of the notion of "identification", Putnam's theory cannot be regarded as an account of what it is for a predicate to be correctly applied to an object or instance of some kind. As I have interpreted Putnam, he is drawing attention to certain contingent facts about our use of natural kind predicates, not giving a theory of what it is for a natural kind predicate to be correctly applied to an object.

One way to avoid mentioning what is identified within a community as belonging to a kind, while at the same time retaining an indexical element, would be to hold that the relation of essential similarity holds between whatever objects are, in the Kripkean sense, causal ancestors of the present use of a natural kind predicate, and those objects which have the same essential properties. Such an account, however, would also fail to be a theory of reference for natural kinds. One reason for this is the same as the one given for why Kripke's account of naming failed to be a theory of reference for proper names: elucidation of the notion of a causal ancestor necessitates mention of an intention to refer to the same kind of thing. The appropriate causal ancestor of our use of the term "electron" would clearly not be Stoney's, for he did not use "electron" to refer to any kind of particle at all! To take another example, early users of the term "gold" could not distinguish real gold from "fool's gold", i.e., from iron pyrites, so again the appropriate causal ancestor has to be traced using some other theory. The extension of natural kind predicates can change, just as the reference of proper names can. A second reason why such an account will not do as a theory of reference for natural kinds is that, where theoretical properties are involved, a change in theory means a change in those properties regarded as essential. A cluster theory, however, can explain both of these features.

5

The account in perspective

In Chapter 1, I posed four interconnected questions which, I argued, a realist would have to answer in order to support his account of the growth of scientific knowledge. Having answered questions (3) and (4), and discussed how to interpret the language of previous theorists, we are now in a position to sum up our answer to the second, to the question:

> (2) How can we discover which objects belong to the extension of a natural kind predicate as that predicate is used within a linguistic community?

The key to our answer is that we have to determine what beliefs members of the linguistic community who used the predicate had about things to which they thought it could be correctly applied. We need to look at what Johannsen (the biologist who coined the term "gene") and those following him believed about what they called genes, at what our ancestors believed about whales, at what beliefs Bohr held about the things he called electrons in 1911, and so on. Of course, it will not always be the case that our predecessors used the same term that we do for a given natural kind (think here of Stoney calling the electric charge on a hydrogen ion in electrolysis an 'electron'), although when we begin to interpret their theory or language we might at first assume that they do.

The data on which we primarily concentrate in our interpretation are the sentences accepted as true by members of the linguistic community in question. If we wish to interpret a language, then our aim is to establish a theory of truth for that language; if we wish to interpret a scientific theory, then our aim is to establish a theory of truth for sentences of the scientific theory. With regard to the latter case, however, it must be remembered that any theory of truth for a part of a language must cohere with a theory of truth for the whole. As we have seen, the more theoretical sentences interrelate with the less theoretical to form the network of language.

To begin with, we have to assume that members of the community are correct, from our point of view, as often as possible; hence the assumption about their using a natural kind predicate to describe the same sort of thing that we use it to describe. In maximizing agreement in this way we attribute to them many of our own beliefs. Unless we thereby obtain some purchase on the notion of meaning we cannot begin interpretation proper.

First-order logic is attributed to members of the community. Working with those sentences always held true or always held false, and valid patterns of inference, we fit our orthodox logic to the language being interpreted. Having settled matters of logical form, we turn to the most observational sentences, i.e., to those whose truth-value bears the most obvious relation to changes in the environment. To give a theory of truth for a language is to state a procedure that will generate, for any sentence of the language, a T-sentence that is true. In the first place we gather evidence for those T-sentences where the object language sentence is most observational. Here we are helped by the inferential links between more and less observational sentences. There is also likely to be a vast amount of primary and secondary linguistic information available, both in interpreting a language as a whole and also in interpreting a scientific theory. Finally, where we are concentrating on a theory of a scientific community, there is the other non-linguistic physical evidence afforded by an examination of any scientific instruments that have been handed down to us.

As we interpret we shall also be guided by a causal constraint on possible attributions of extensions to predicates: members of the linguistic community under consideration must have been in an appropriate causal relation to things of whatever kind we decide they were applying a predicate to (a similar constraint holds for the attribution of referents to singular terms). For us to say that Bohr was talking about electrons, he must have performed experiments which made essential use of them, or at least have been acquainted with the results obtained by others who had performed such experiments. Members of the natural kind – and here it is we who decide, on the basis of our own "theory of nature" what the members are – have to be (causally) "at the root of" beliefs if these beliefs are to be properly described as being about things of that kind. Here we see the importance to the realist of the connection between words and the world. In order for members of a linguistic community C to be interpreted as using a natural kind predicate "φ" to describe ψs, it is necessary that there be some causal connection between ψs and members of C, namely that between ψs and what is believed about the things called "φ"s within C. This is a point rightly emphasized by those who argue for a causal account of reference.

In the light of all this further information, and the suggested interpretations, it might prove necessary to revise, in certain places, our original charitable assumptions. This in turn might lead us to alter some of our interpretations, and so on. In general there is no ground for assuming that there will be just one admissible theory of truth for a language on the basis of the available data (or even on the basis of all the possible data in Quine's sense). To return to the Quinean idiom, sentence translation may well turn out not to be determinate. This is not a cause for concern to the realist, for he is satisfied with *optimal* translation, translation that is consistent with all the evidence; he need not insist on there being *perfect* or *unique* translation. What would be a cause for his concern would be if such a lack of determinacy implied that we cannot scrutinize the reference or extension of terms of the object language. We have found no argument to support this implication, and, as I argued in Chapters 2 and 3, even Quine's doctrine of the indeterminacy of translation of sentences is logically independent of his doctrine of the inscrutability of reference of terms.

Applying this strategy to particular cases, the realist can hope to discover the extension of a natural kind predicate as it is used within a given linguistic community. In general, how successful he will then be in explaining the progress of science is not something that can be specified in advance; it is a contingent matter. There may be many cases where he cannot establish the extensions of predicates from previous scientific theories. And even where he can it might turn out that subsequent or competing theories are *not* about the same things. In order to better appreciate this, let me present three case studies.

2 ATOMS AND MOLECULES

In 1808, John Dalton published Part 1 of his *A New System of Chemical Philosophy* in which he propounded a theory of chemistry based on a molecular theory of matter. The postulates which formed the basis of his molecular theory were essentially satisfactory and correct. Unfortunately, however, as the basis for a chemical theory of gases they were not in themselves sufficient to make possible a calculation of atomic weights, which was necessary in order to show in what way atoms of different gases were different. To fill this lacuna, Dalton boldly assumed an arbitrary set of maxims which amounted to a rule of greatest simplicity with respect to the ratios in which elements combine to form compound molecules:

If there are two bodies, A and B, which are disposed to combine, the following is the order in which the combinations may take place, beginning with the most simple, namely:
1 atom of A + 1 atom of B = 1 atom of C, binary.
1 atom of A + 2 atoms of B = 1 atom of D, ternary. . . .
The following general rules may be adopted as guides in all our investigations respecting chemical synthesis.
1st. When only one combination of two bodies can be obtained, it must be presumed to be a *binary* one, unless some cause appear to the contrary. (1808: 218)

The trouble with these maxims is that they brought Dalton's theory of gases into conflict with some carefully determined experimental results of the French chemist Gay-Lussac. These were encapsulated in his Law of Combining Volumes: when gases react chemically, the proportions by volume measured at the same temperature and pressure bear simple whole number relations to each other, and the volumes of the products (if gaseous) measured under the same conditions also bear simple whole number relations to the volumes of the reacting gases. When oxygen and hydrogen react to form water, for example, one volume of oxygen and two volumes of hydrogen yield two volumes of water vapour.

If Dalton had accepted that there is some simple relation between volumes of different gases and the number of 'atoms' they contain, he might have been able to explain these results. But he had at least three reasons for not doing so. In the first place he thought that 'atoms' of different elements have different sizes, and so believed that different numbers of them would occupy the same volume. Secondly, there would have been cases where, in order to reconcile his maxims with Gay-Lussac's law, he would have to have accepted that certain of what he regarded as atoms – oxygen molecules, for example – were composed of two like parts. From the beginning, though, Dalton had been impressed by Newton's work on electricity and magnetism, and he adopted Newton's model of air as an elastic fluid constituted of like atoms which repel each other by a force increasing as their distance diminishes. "Like repels like" was, for Dalton, a universal truth. Finally, Dalton claimed to have experimental evidence of his own that conflicted with Gay-Lussac's law. Thus, Dalton remained steadfastly opposed to the law.

In 1811, Amadeo Avogadro, an Italian physicist, published an obscure paper entitled 'Essay on a manner of determining the relative masses of the elementary molecules of bodies, and the proportions in which they enter into these compounds'. He pointed out that to *deny* that the number of molecules contained in a given volume at a given temperature and pressure were the same for different gases would have made it virtually impossible to account for the observed regularities of reactions. Avogadro went on to propound a hypothesis, now referred to as his law, that equal volumes of all gases, under the same conditions, contain equal numbers of molecules. He added, as a corollary to this, what we should now express by saying that the molecules of elementary gases were usually composed of more than one atom. On the basis of the hypothesis it was possible not only to explain Gay-Lussac's results but also to provide a method of finding true molecular formulae without arbitrary maxims of simplicity. The advances made in the chemistry of the late nineteenth century were the result.

How does all this illustrate our problem? Well, we have two theories about the molecular composition of gases: Dalton's and Avogadro's. Let us denote the former as T^1 and the latter as T^2. From the point of view of our own science, it seems natural to say that one salient difference between T^1 and T^2 is that T^2 distinguishes atoms from molecules whereas T^1 does not. Of course, it is not quite as simple as this. Although Dalton uses "atom" and "molecule" more or less interchangeably, he also uses the terms "ultimate particle" and "simple elementary particle" to denote atoms or molecules of compounds. Avogadro employs a wide range of terminology as well, distinguishing atoms of elements from molecules of elements and molecules of compounds (1811: 28, fn. 2). And this is only how we *would* characterize their vocabulary *if* we had some way of comparing terms from different theories.

For the sake of simplicity, I shall concentrate on Dalton's term 'atom', which he uses in presenting his maxims of simplicity, and Avogadro's term 'molecule', which occurs in his hypothesis. Were they, in using these terms, talking about the same things or not? How are we to decide? It seems plain that when Dalton uses the term "atom" to talk about the elementary particles of gases, he is referring to what Avogadro and modern chemists would term "molecules". Because of this it seems plain also that the claim Dalton would make using the statement "No atoms of gases are composed of two like particles" is directly contradicted by the claim Avogadro and modern chemists would make using the statement "Some molecules of gases are composed of two like particles". And it is this which inclines us to say that Dalton's theory was factually incorrect, i.e., that it led to false statements about how the world is.

The realist's strategy here is to try to establish that "atom of a gas" for Dalton had the same extension as "molecule of a gas" for Avogadro. Let us substitute the letters "P" and "Q" respectively for these predicates. Remembering our discussion in Chapter 1 of the formal sense of the first of the four crucial questions, we may say that what he tries to establish is the truth of the statement:

(i)   "P" and "Q" are co-extensive.

If this can be established, then the two claims may be written in logical form using the language of T^2 – the language in which "Q" is used – as

(ii) $(x)\ (Qx \supset \sim\!Dx)$
(iii) $(\exists x)\ (Qx\ \&\ Dx)$

where "D" is the predicate of T^2 "is composed of two like particles", and where it is assumed that there are some things of which "Q" is true. From this the realist can conclude that they offered contradictory accounts of the same objects – what Avogadro's theory identified as molecules of gases. Since we now accept most of the things Avogadro said, this provides the basis for a criticism of Dalton's theory; (iii) is true and hence (ii) is false; Dalton's maxims also were mistaken. So some of Dalton's beliefs about *molecules* were incorrect.

We ended our consideration of question (1) in Chapter 1 by wondering how we could obtain sufficient information to establish as true statements like (i) above. This led to question (2), an epistemological question of how we can discover which objects belong to the extension of some particular natural kind predicate used within a linguistic community. This in turn led to question (3), which asked a question of conceptual analysis: what is it for a natural kind predicate to have an extension? Our answer to question (3) depended on the theory of interpretation given in Chapter 3. What it means in the case of interpreting Dalton's theory is that the extension of his term 'atom' is a function of what he believed about those things to which he applied the term. This will be forthcoming from a theory of truth for the sentences of Dalton's theory of gases. Of course this theory forms only part of his general theory of chemistry, which itself is given by only a subset of the set of sentences held true by Dalton.

In accordance with the principle of charity, we assume that Dalton was right as often as possible. As interpretation proceeds, this solves the problem of the interdependence of belief and meaning by holding belief constant while meanings are unpacked. A second assumption is that Dalton's language is based on quantification theory. This assumption, and the subsequent attempt to fit our logic onto Dalton's language, should not, of course, raise any practical problems since the idiom is not that of *radical* interpretation. This paves the way for modelling a theory of interpretation on a Tarskian theory of truth. The important question now is how determinate the resultant interpretation of Dalton's predicates will be.

As a result of our work in Chapter 2, we have no reason to suppose that the reference or extension of any of Dalton's terms will be inscrutable. Following Quine and Davidson, we also have no reason to expect any difficulty in interpreting the more observational of Dalton's statements. What remains is for us to get from these "bits of evidence" to a "rich concept" of interpretation that will help us decide whether statement (i) above is true. In Chapter 3 we found reason to suspect the doubts Quine had about this step; they seem to rely on a firm distinction between the observational and the theoretical, a distinction brought into question by, among other things, Quine's own network model of theories. Attention was also drawn to the vast amount of primary and secondary linguistic evidence that we would have in this case. We noted that, as a consequence of our being able to interpret the more observational of Dalton's statements, we could discover from his laboratory notebooks, published papers reporting his experiments, and scientific apparatus he was known to have used, what his techniques of chemical analysis and synthesis were. Therefore, when Dalton says that 'atoms' are irreducible given the known techniques, we can repeat his experiments if needs be. Here we are also guided by a general causal constraint to the effect that for, say, his 'atom' to be taken as co-extensive with our "molecule" there must have been a causal connection between molecules and what Dalton believed about the things he called 'atoms'.

Let us suppose that all of this information leads us to interpret Dalton's term 'atom' as being coextensive with our predicate "is a particle of a gas which is not divisible by chemical means". This might be expressed more formally as:

(A) For any *a*, 'atom' is true of *a* in Dalton's theory of gases if and only if *a* is a particle of a gas which is not divisible by chemical means.

We now have to go back to interpret Avogadro's theory to see if we can obtain a similar statement for his term 'molecule'. There can be little doubt, though, that this will *not* be forthcoming. As I noted in my introduction of this case, our present-day molecular theory of gases has taken over many of Avogadro's principal ideas. In particular, chemists have come to regard his hypothesis that equal volumes of all gases, under the same conditions, contain equal numbers of molecules as a fundamental law. Furthermore, it is accepted that molecules of gases often divide in chemical reactions, for example, where diatomic oxygen molecules divide, each to unite with a molecule of hydrogen to form a molecule of water. But this need not constitute a serious set-back to the project of showing that Avogadro's theory was a rival, then a successor, to Dalton's. For it is always possible to revise, in certain places, our charitable assumption about Dalton's beliefs. And indeed, the more incorrect we intuitively judge a previous theory the more frequently we might expect to revise our initial assignments of truth-values to sentences. So from the point of view of an alternative to (A) we may judge Dalton to be wrong when he said that 'atoms' were not divisible by chemical means. Such an alternative, for which there is ample justification in Dalton's *A New System of Chemical Philosophy*, is:

(A′) For any *a*, 'atom' is true of *a* in Dalton's theory of gases if and only if *a* is a smallest particle of a gas to have all the chemical properties of the gas.

Moreover, work carried out since Avogadro's time has shown that:

(A″) For any *a*, 'molecule' is true of *a* in Avogadro's theory of gases if and only if *a* is a smallest particle of a gas to have all the chemical properties of the gas.

Since (A′) and (A″) are both contained in the same language, it follows that what Dalton called 'atoms', Avogadro called 'molecules'; or, more formally, that:

(A‴) For any *a*, 'atom' is true of *a* in Dalton's theory of gases if and only if 'molecule' is true of *a* in Avogadro's theory of gases.

And this will be so even though many of the beliefs held by Dalton and Avogadro about their subject-matter might be different. That is, it will be so even though the senses they attached to the terms they used might be different.

The complex path leading to (A''') constitutes an answer to a particular instance of my original question (1) of Chapter 1. This is the primary question in the realist's account of the growth of science. If (A') and (A'') are true, then Dalton and Avogadro were talking about the same things. Perhaps the most difficult task is establishing that what Dalton and Avogadro regarded as the chemical properties of a gas were more or less the same. Naturally this would itself involve interpretation that would suggest statements of the same form as (A') and (A''). But notice that "chemical properties" is a less theoretical, more tractable term than "molecule" (or "atom"). We might therefore expect to be able to make more use of laboratory notebooks, observation reports, and also of the kind of information afforded by examining the apparatus used by Dalton when considered along with the causal constraint. In the end, though, what has to be emphasized is that the success of the realist's account of the growth of scientific knowledge depends crucially on the evidence he has available in each case. That science does progress by giving more successful theories about the same things is in this sense a contingent claim.

So far in this book I have concentrated on cases where the relevant scientific predicate is a natural kind predicate and where one's intuitive view is that subsequent theories are about the same things. I have argued for a number of philosophical points which make sense of this intuition. The next two cases I shall consider are, in their own ways, rather different from this. The first is one where we now tend to say that there is nothing of the kind postulated by earlier theorists, and the second is one where the relevant predicate is not a natural kind predicate.

3 PHLOGISTON

The first case turns on the difference between two sorts of error we might wish to ascribe to our ancestors: a predicate they used failing to have any extension at all according to *our* conceptual scheme, and its having an extension but their holding false beliefs about what they correctly applied it to. I have already mentioned several cases, besides the one we have just considered, which appear to be of the latter kind: Bohr thought that at all times electrons have precise positions and momenta, Muller believed that genes were composed of proteins, Ptolemy held that the other planets revolved around the earth, and so on. Less attention has been paid to those cases where we now assign a null extension to predicates from previous scientific theories: from our point of view there is no phlogiston, no luminiferous ether surrounding the earth, no caloric surrounding atoms, and so on. Is there a clear dividing line between these two sorts of cases? How do we decide between them?

We have to be careful here to distinguish between questions of the form "What, according to *us*, is the extension of the predicate 'φ'?" and questions of the form "Did members of linguistic community C succeed in describing anything when *they* used the term 'φ'?". According to us, the predicate "phlogiston" has null extension: there is no such thing as phlogiston, those who believed that there was were mistaken. Nevertheless, chemists during most of the eighteenth century described the results of some of their experiments using the predicate, and in so doing were thought by their contemporaries to have made true statements. Thus, suppose that one such chemist offers the following report of a familiar laboratory observation:

(OR1) On addition of oil of vitriol to granulated zinc, evolution of phlogiston was observed.

Such a report would have been accepted as true by other chemists of the time. To us it seems obvious what the chemist in fact observed, namely, the evolution of hydrogen on addition of sulphuric acid to granulated zinc. (We can interpret their laboratory notebooks.) Yet if we fail to distinguish between the above questions – if we fall victim to what a relativist may characterize as "the chauvinism of time" (Jardine 1978: 107) – then since there is (tenseless) no such thing as phlogiston, there can be no such event as an evolution of phlogiston, and so the report cannot be said to describe any event at all.

Such failure to distinguish leads to two problems. The first is that not being able to assign the value "true" to many of their observation reports conflicts with the principle of charity. We might now say that there is no such thing as phlogiston, but if we hold that it follows from this that the predicate lacked an extension for early eighteenth-century chemists, then our interpretation of their science will diverge in countless places from their own understanding. The sort of generalization which reports like (OR1) will tend to support is:

    (x) (if x is a member of the community of early eighteenth-century chemists then (x holds "OR1" true if and only if x observes an evolution of hydrogen when sulphuric acid is added to granulated zinc)).

This in turn supports the T-sentence:

    "OR1" is true in the language of early eighteenth-century chemistry for a speaker x if and only if x observes an evolution of hydrogen when sulphuric acid is added to granulated zinc.

But neither the generalization nor the T-sentence are supported if we refuse to assign an extension to the predicate "phlogiston" as used by them.

The second problem is related to the first and can also be stated briefly. If such observation reports fail to describe anything at all, then the widespread agreement by chemists of the time over what truth-value they are to be assigned must strike us as nothing short of *miraculous*. How could they agree if there was not anything there for them to correctly apply their predicates to? This point is made by Nick Jardine in a recent paper (1978), where he levels it against a principle for making retrospective assignments of extension which Putnam calls the 'principle of benefit of the doubt' (Putnam 1978: Lecture I). According to Putnam's principle, we are permitted to identify the extension of a predicate "ψ" of our science with that of a simple predicate "φ" (like "gene" or "atom") of a past science provided only that the descriptions which protagonists of the past science used to characterize φs would, when 'reasonably reformulated', characterize ψs. This principle, says Putnam, would allow us to 'assign a referent to "gravitational field" in Newtonian theory from the standpoint of relativity theory (though not to "ether" or "phlogiston"); a referent to Mendel's "gene" (*sic*) from the standpoint of present-day molecular biology; and a referent to Dalton's "atom" from the standpoint of quantum mechanics' (1978: 22). What Jardine claims is that accepting this principle requires us to acknowledge, in cases like "phlogiston", that there can be miracles! He also sees another difficulty in its acceptance. The principle forces us into a dilemma when it comes to interpreting simple predicates of a past science. *Either* we must equate its extension with that of a simple predicate of our own science, *or* we must admit that it has null extension. It forces us to accept that there is a clear dividing line between the two sorts of cases.

Seeking to avoid the postulation of miracles, Jardine is led to argue 'that it is a precondition for assignment of extension to the predicates of a past science that that assignment be such as to make many such observation reports [as (OR1)] come out true' (1978: 112). We are well placed to agree with Jardine here, for not only do we too wish to avoid talking of miracles, we also have to defend a principle of charity underlying our theory of interpretation. Let me now explain how what I have said earlier in this book meets Jardine's precondition.

The theory of reference for natural kind predicates that I adumbrated in Chapter 4 was a theory of what it is for an object a to belong to a natural kind predicate "φ" *as that predicate is used within a linguistic community* C. In keeping with this, the specification of the extensions of predicates in statements (A) – (A''') from the last section was accomplished by using a three-place relation holding between a term, a set of objects and a theory. If it should turn out that, say, certain occurrences of hydrogen satisfy a suitable majority of those descriptions which could be consistently attributed to phlogiston on the basis of what was believed by early eighteenth-century chemists about phlogiston, then this theory of reference will reckon those instances to form part of the extension of "phlogiston" as used by early eighteenth-century chemists. The realist could thus hope to discover that the following is true:

(B) For any a, "phlogiston" is true of a in early eighteenth-century chemistry if a is an occurrence of hydrogen resulting from the addition of sulphuric acid to granulated zinc.

Another observation report on which Georgian chemists also agreed is that phlogiston is evolved when certain substances are burnt in air. What in fact happens, according to us, is that oxygen combines with the substances. Using the same procedure as was used to discover the truth of (B) above, the realist could hope to establish as true:

(B') For any a, "phlogiston" is true of a in early eighteenth-century chemistry if a is an occurrence of oxygen which combines with a substance when it is burnt in air.

Combining (B) and (B') he then obtains:

(B'') For any a, "phlogiston" is true of a in early eighteenth-century chemistry if a is an occurrence of matter which is

115

either hydrogen resulting from the addition of sulphuric acid to granulated zinc, *or* oxygen combining with a substance when it is burnt.

Now as a matter of fact Georgian chemists believed that several other experiments led to the production of phlogiston. Once these have been accounted for, the realist, as Jardine also notes (1978: 122), will specify the extension of their simple predicate using a *complex disjunctive* predicate. That is, what he finally comes to accept as true will be something of the form:

(B''') For any *a*, "phlogiston" is true of *a* in early eighteenth-century chemistry if and only if *a* is an occurrence of matter which is *either* hydrogen resulting from the addition of sulphuric acid to granulated zinc, *or* oxygen combining with a substance when it is burnt, *or* . . .

Such a retrospective assignment of extension ensures that (OR1), and other well-established reports like it, are assigned the value "true" in the language of eighteenth-century chemists.

It is instructive to consider this notion of a complex disjunctive predicate along with Field's concept of partial denotation (1973). When I discussed the latter in Chapter 4, I suggested that although it could not properly take the place of the more fundamental concept of plain denotation, it could usefully be considered as a supplement to it in cases where a theory such as that contained in my (3'C) could not resolve two or more alternatives for the extension of a predicate which were equally supported by the evidence from interpretation. The "phlogiston" example seems to be just such a case. "Phlogiston" as used by Georgian chemists did not simply denote certain occurrences of hydrogen or oxygen; it *partially denoted* both.

A further advantage of (B''') is that it enables the realist to avoid the dilemma forced on one who accepts Putnam's 'principle of benefit of the doubt'. He is free to recognize that contemporary chemists have no one simple predicate to which they assign the same extension as was assigned by early-eighteenth-century chemists to their simple predicate "phlogiston", without thereby committing himself to the conclusion that their predicate has a null extension. More generally, it is to be expected that the theory of interpretation which I have presented, based as it is on a cluster theory of reference, will always urge us to assign a non-empty extension to predicates of previous theories provided we can detect a consistent use of the predicate. If we repeatedly end up with inconsistent assignments of beliefs to users of the predicate, then we have no reason for thinking that there are things to which they believed it could be correctly applied. Jardine suggests that Gassendi's predicate 'atom' might turn out to be such a case (1978: 123); perhaps, for reasons I shall mention shortly, "phlogiston" as used by *late*-eighteenth-century chemists would be another.[1] But where a predicate is used consistently within a community there are good intuitive and methodological reasons for assigning an extension to it relative to that community.

In between these two possibilities there appears to be a third: we may be unsure, given the vagaries of interpretation, whether or not a predicate was used consistently. We might be able to vary assignments of truth-values to sentences and so specify different extensions for their predicates. Perhaps the earlier theorists were not as truthful as we at first charitably assumed; perhaps the evidence at hand will be just too thin to resolve the matter. In such cases the realist has to conclude that the extension of the predicate is underdetermined by the available evidence. There is thus no clear dividing line between cases involving false beliefs and those involving non-instantiated predicates.

Such a construal of realism contrasts with the inflexible doctrines that have previously been accorded that epithet. Take, for example, Richard Rorty's vivid description of the realist as holding that there were determinate moments in the past when language threw out a fresh grappling hook and succeeded in fastening onto a piece of the world (1976: 326–7). By making the success of the realist's account of scientific progress for any one change of theory contingent on the evidence we now have available for interpretation, we can appreciate that there need be no such determinacy. The scientist's hooks may grapple with one piece of the world several times (Bohr's electron theory and that of the present day), or with several different pieces (phlogiston theory and modern chemistry), and may not always do so successfully (Gassendi's atomic theory). The realist therefore need not, as Rorty claims, adhere to a sharp distinction between false belief and non-instantiation. As he himself is at pains to point out, there may even be cases where the pragmatist reply of "no fact of the matter" is warranted, though according to my account this will be as a result of empirical investigation, not of *a priori* reasoning. Furthermore, it has been my contention that a realist needs a theory of reference to substantiate his position and to make sense of such

---

[1] In general, at times of crisis (in the sense of Kuhn 1970), when there are frequent contradictions between theory and observation, we might often be obliged to assign a null extension.

claims about our ancestors. Far from his reliance on such a theory being the blind alley suggested by Rorty (1980: Ch. 6), I believe it is a necessary precursor to any complete understanding.

The account I have given of how we should assign extensions to predicates of past theories leads to the following picture of the growth of scientific knowledge. Suppose there is a theory T^1 which contains a natural kind predicate "P" and which comes to be replaced by theory T^2 containing natural kind predicate "Q". The question arises as to whether those things described as Ps by users of T^1 are the same as those described as Qs by users of T^2. According to my account, an affirmative answer should be given to this question when a suitable majority of those descriptions believed to be true of Ps by users of T^1 also constitutes a suitable majority of those descriptions believed to be true of Qs by users of T^2. As an example of this I suggested, in the previous section, that what Avogadro described as molecules, Dalton had described as atoms; the "suitable majority of descriptions" being "is a smallest particle of a gas to have all the chemical properties of the gas". In this section I have considered the case of phlogiston theory. After Lavoisier and the discovery of oxygen, phlogiston theory was given up. According to post-eighteenth-century chemists, no one thing satisfied a suitable majority of those descriptions which *they* could consistently attribute to phlogiston on the basis of what *they* believed. Probably the main reason for their having adopted this view is that as experimental techniques improved towards the end of the eighteenth century it was demonstrated that, since all metals gained weight on calcination, phlogiston, which was thought to cause calcination by being evolved, must have negative weight. But the idea of an element having negative weight seemed then, as it has ever since, to be of dubious intelligibility. There was no question, moreover, of this difficulty being overcome. It was not just a matter of one false belief among many true ones. Phlogiston's having negative weight was a consequence of the theory itself and not something which could be shelved or left for future science to resolve. The theory was abandoned and no one simple predicate with the same extension was subsequently used.

None of this, however, prevents us from interpreting the language, and making sense of the actions, of early- eighteenth-century chemists in the way suggested. The realist need not be a chauvinist. He can make sense of errors on the part of earlier scientists. He can also render intelligible such statements as "In the dark ages they talked about witches, although in fact such people were mainly schizophrenics", but to discuss this would take me too far afield.

4 MASS

The final example I want to discuss leads us, in a sense, back to our starting point, for it is one of the main examples considered by Feyerabend in arguing against accounts of the growth of science which were based on the notion of the reduction of an early theory to a later one. From Chapter 1 we recall that he discusses a number of purported reductions of this kind which Nagel claimed to be in accordance with the conditions of derivability – 'the laws of the reduced theory must be logically derivable from the reducing theory together with certain coordinating definitions' – and meaning invariance – 'the meanings of the theoretical terms contained in the derived laws are the same as those of the terms as they occur in the reduced theory'. As an example of reduction where meanings are supposed to have remained invariant, Feyerabend considers the replacement of classical mechanics by relativity theory, concentrating on the term "mass" as it occurs in each (1965: 168 ff.). The essential difference between the two theories is that classical mechanics assumes that the mass of a particle is constant whereas in relativity theory it is said to be proportional to a frame of reference. According to Feyerabend there is a change of meaning here because classical mass is a property of an object itself whereas relativistic mass is a relation, and because (apparently) incompatible equations about mass hold in the two theories.

I noted in Section 1 of Chapter 1 certain difficulties which arise with Feyerabend's position, particularly with regard to claims about the incompatibility of incommensurable theories. Part of the problem with Feyerabend's position, as with those which he attacks, is an apparent reliance on a flimsy notion of meaning. Aiming to avoid this, while at the same time preserving a sense of scientific progress, I turned to what a realist might say in response. The nub of the realist's view is that competing or successive scientific theories are often theories about the same kinds of thing. Scientists usually act in accordance with this view when formulating new theories and, says the realist, science progresses as a result. We have seen that the realist cannot fully abjure meaning – he makes use of the notion in

119

explaining how we come to understand what theories are about. But he is not committed to the condition of meaning invariance. All that a realist need claim remain invariant are the extensions of predicates.

In discussing the realist's general view I concentrated on natural kind predicates. One interesting feature of them is that they do not usually admit of simple, precise definitions. To connote this feature I adopted the expression "cluster term", which Putnam uses to describe these predicates. The point is that natural kind predicates are defined using a cluster of properties, not all of which need be true of an object in order for it to be reckoned one of the kind. Of some relevance to the present context is the fact that Putnam's intention, in first introducing the expression, is to use it to characterize terms such as "energy", "mass", "temperature", and so on which frequently occur in scientific laws. These he calls 'law-cluster concepts' (1962: 52). According to Putnam:

Law-cluster concepts are constituted not by a bundle of properties as are the typical general names like "man" and "crow", but by a cluster of laws which, as it were, determine the identity of the concept. The concept "energy" is an excellent example of a law-cluster concept. It enters into a great many laws. It plays a great many roles, and these laws and inference roles constitute its meaning collectively, not individually. (1962: 52)

This feature, which goes to make such terms law-cluster concepts, leads Putnam to draw the following conclusion about theory change:

In general, any one law can be abandoned without destroying the identity of the law-cluster concept involved, just as a man can be irrational from birth, or can have a growth of feathers all over his body, without ceasing to be a man. Applying this to our example – "kinetic energy" = "kinetic" + "energy" – the kinetic energy of a particle is literally the energy due to its motion. The extension of the term "kinetic energy" has not changed. If it had, the extension of the term "energy" would have to have changed. But the extension of the term "energy" has not changed. The forms of energy and their behaviour are the same as they always were, and they are what physicists talked about before and after Einstein. On the other hand, I want to suggest that the term "energy" is not one of which it is *happy* to ask, What is its intension? The term "intension" suggests the idea of a single defining character or a single defining law, and this is not the model on which concepts like energy are to be construed. (1962: 52)

If Putnam is right here then this is of great importance to the realist in the face of the present problem. It suggests that he can accept that the meaning of the term "mass" might not have stayed the same in the change from classical mechanics to relativistic mechanics but that the extension of the term has. What might be a cause for scepticism, however, is Putnam's bold claim that 'the forms of energy and their behaviour are the same as they always were'. What exactly does he mean by 'the forms of energy and their behaviour'? And how are we to decide what the behaviour of something is if not through consideration of the laws it is said to obey? Before discussing the problem further, let me make some more general remarks.

One important difference between natural kind predicates and law-cluster terms is that the former are used to refer to things of a kind whereas the latter are used to express properties that things have. That is, law-cluster terms are typically used to express measurements. For this reason they are more correctly said to be two(or more)-place predicates; natural kind predicates, on the other hand, are one-place. The classical mass of a particle, for example, is expressed by a functional relation between that particle and a number. This contrast underlies the one Putnam expresses in terms of a difference between 'a bundle of properties' and 'a cluster of laws'.

Since terms for measurements are two(or more)-place predicates, their extensions consist of ordered pairs (or n-tuples). It would appear, then, that the realist's claim of "reference invariance", applied to them, amounts to the claim that the law-cluster predicates of successive theories have the same sets of ordered pairs (n-tuples) in their extensions. Where before we asked questions like whether the extension of Newton's 'planet' was the same as the extension of ours, we now have to ask whether the values assigned to, say, "the mass of planet x" within Newton's theory of gravitation correspond to values assigned by any predicate of ours of the form "the ψ of planet x". It might be the case that we do not believe some things about "ψ" which Newtonians believed about "mass", but in point of extension they have to be the same.

This contrast between predicates the extensions of which are things and predicates the extensions of which are ordered n-tuples suggests a difference in the intuitive appeal of the realist's account of theory change for the different types of case. In the first the realist can say, for example, that Mendel and Muller were both talking about just these things, genes; or that Ptolemy and Newton were talking about just this planet, Venus. In the second, though, he seems to be limited to saying things like that Newton and Einstein *would* both

121

have assigned the value 6 to this object. The measurements have to be made; the kinds of thing that are measured are already there.

The difference here can be made clearer if we concentrate on the notion of a causal relation. This formed an important part of my account of how we can discover what the extension of a natural kind predicate is. I argued that in order for members of some linguistic community to be said to use a natural kind predicate "φ" to describe ψs, they (or their ancestors) must have been causally related to ψs. Numbers, however, do not stand in causal relations to people (or to anything for that matter). Ptolemy and Newton might both have observed the planet Venus – it reflected light from the sun onto their retinas – just as Dalton and Avogadro both observed the behaviour of gases. But there is no sense in saying that Newton or Einstein could have observed 6 or its effects (though of course they could have observed a pointer indicating "6" on a scale). This difference, I believe, largely accounts for the special problems associated with theory change where the relevant predicate is a law-cluster term. The connection between words and the world is more complex.

Returning to the "mass" example, this has been discussed at length by Hartry Field in his paper 'Theory change and the indeterminacy of reference' (1973). As the title suggests, Field thinks it has something to do with a doctrine of Quine's (exactly which doctrine is a point discussed below). This is made clear from the outset where he states his general thesis as being 'that considerations about scientific revolutions show that many scientific terms are *referentially indeterminate* – there is no fact of the matter as to what they denote (if they are singular terms) or as to what their extension is (if they are general terms)' (1973: 462). His sole argument in support of this thesis rests on the example we have been discussing.

The essence of Field's claim is this. In relativity physics there are two properties – *proper mass* and *relativistic mass* – each of which resembles classical mass, though in different respects. Thus, the relativistic mass of a particle, when multiplied by its velocity, is equivalent to its momentum; this is not so for proper mass. The proper mass of a particle, on the other hand, is the same in all frames of reference; its relativistic mass is not. So no matter which property is chosen as the "successor" to classical mass, classical physics must be judged wrong in some respect or other when viewed from the standpoint of relativity physics. Moreover, according to Field there is no fact of the matter as regards which choice should be made. His

122

conclusion is that we have an instance of 'the indeterminacy of reference'.

It seems to me that the initial reaction to this argument by anyone with some understanding of modern physics would be that Field is plainly wrong. Almost every modern textbook on physics goes to some length to point out that what Newton called "mass" modern physicists call "proper mass" or "rest mass". But the question remains, what substance can be given to this claim? In a recent reply to Field, John Earman holds that there is an 'exact parallelism' between some central principles of Newtonian and special relativistic mechanics (1977). To see the parallelism it is necessary to formulate both theories in what Earman calls 'a four-dimensional, intrinsic (i.e., coordinate free) form' (1977: 535; cf. Earman & Friedman 1973). The three principles central to Newtonian mechanics can then be written as:

(N1) m_n is a scalar invariant
(N2) $P_n = m_n V_n$
(N3) $F_n = m_n A_n$

where m_n, P_n, V_n, F_n, A_n are, respectively, the Newtonian mass, the Newtonian four-momentum, four-velocity, four-force and four-acceleration. Earman's point is that in the special theory of relativity there are exact analogues (R1), (R2), (R3) of (N1), (N2), (N3) with proper mass m_0 in place of m_n, the relativistic four-momentum P_r in place of P_n, etc. So it would seem that while Field was right to say that in the usual formulation of the special theory, proper mass multiplied by velocity does not equal momentum, the theory can be written in an alternative 'four-dimensional, intrinsic form' in which the equation does hold.

Let us accept that Earman is right about there being this 'exact parallelism'. Why should it convince us that classical mass is to be identified with proper mass? Earman's reply relies on its being the case that (N1) – (N3) and (R1) – (R3) occupy positions of great importance within their respective theories. He claims that 'if any tenets are central to the Newtonian concept of mass and the relativistic concept of proper mass, it is (N1) – (N3) and (R1) – (R3) respectively' (1977: 536). What is philosophically interesting about this is the idea that in cases of theory comparison where the relevant predicate is a law–cluster predicate, we should pay particular attention to the structure of the laws stated in the theories. This suggests a further criterion which could be used in resolving problems arising in such cases. We might phrase it as follows: where there is a *prima facie* choice over which predicate from one theory is to be said to have the same extension as a predicate from another, choose the one which would best preserve the mathematical structure between the theories. It will still be the case that, as Field says, classical physics will be judged wrong from the standpoint of relativity physics, but if Earman is right then we can at least see in the latter a successor to the former.

What then becomes of indeterminacy? Even with the added criterion, we have no guarantee that we shall be able to decide precisely how to interpret every statement of Newton's, or, more generally, that we shall always be able to specify the extension of a law-cluster predicate from another theory. But as we noted in the previous section, this sort of case only shows that interpretation can be under-determined by the available evidence, not that it is *in*determinate. And in any case, even if it *were* shown that translation, or interpretation, is indeterminate, it would still not follow that reference is inscrutable. That is, we might not be sure how to interpret a Newtonian assertion like "The mass of a particle is equal to twice its kinetic energy divided by the square of its velocity", even after we have appreciated what Earman has to say. We might even concede that all the available evidence is insufficient to decide its interpretation. Yet none of this would show the extension of Newton's 'mass' to be inscrutable. So Field is wrong on two counts: we need not conclude that there is indeterminacy, and, even if there were, it would not be indeterminacy of *reference*.

Lastly, what about Feyerabend's views? He too has an objection to identifying the extension of "classical mass" with that of "proper mass". In Chapter 1, I reported him as saying 'although both may have the same *numerical value*, they cannot be represented by the same concept' (1965: 169). If this is intended to express the point that not everything said of "mass" in classical physics is accepted as true of "proper mass" in relativity physics, then this might well be accepted by a realist. But this very claim is one that presupposes that the two theories are commensurable, a presupposition of which the realist alone can make sense.

Conclusion

I began Chapter 1 by explaining how an impasse had been reached in contemporary discussion of the problem of scientific progress. This arose from the relativist's challenge to the accounts of progress afforded by positivism and falsificationism. Central to this challenge is the claim that the terms of competing or successive theories are incommensurable, i.e., that there is in principle no way of showing that they mean the same. This shift from what has been traditionally regarded as a problem in the philosophy of science to a problem in the philosophy of language determined the content of the later chapters.

My aim has been to explicate and defend a realist account of the progress of science. Peculiar to this account is a thesis not about meaning but about reference, namely that competing or successive theories are usually about the same things. I have maintained that a necessary condition for making sense of this thesis is a theory of reference for scientific terms. This explains the nature and order of what I characterized as 'four questions for realism':

(1) How can we compare the extensions of relevant natural kind predicates from different scientific theories?

(2) How can we discover which objects belong to the extension of a natural kind predicate as that predicate is used within a linguistic community?

(3) What conditions have to be satisfied by a natural kind predicate "φ" and an object a in order for "φ", as it is used within a linguistic community C, to be correctly applied to a?

(4) Is there a determinate relation of reference between natural kind predicates, as used within linguistic communities, and sets of objects?

I argued that the most obvious way of answering questions (1) – (3) was by first answering each of their successors. But in any event what counts is that the realist must have *some* answer to questions (1) – (3), and this means that he must be able to answer question (4) in the affirmative.

125

In discussing question (4), I concentrated on Quine's doctrine of the inscrutability of reference of terms. I argued that even if we accepted Quine's strictures on radical translation, in particular that the only available evidence was behavioural, he had failed to establish his doctrine. The primary reason for this failure is that he pays insufficient attention to the fine-grained structure of language, to how singular terms and predicates combine to give truth-functional sentences. In Chapters 2 and 3, I also discussed the relation between inscrutability and Quine's other doctrine of the indeterminacy of translation of sentences. I noted that simply because we might be able to show that, say, Dalton had a theory about the molecules of gases, it did not follow that we could determinately translate everything which he said about them. This suggested that scrutability of reference did not imply determinacy of translation, from which it seems to follow that indeterminacy of translation does not imply inscrutability of reference. So an affirmative answer to (4) would not be threatened even if Quine were right about indeterminacy. This provided the background for answers to the less fundamental questions (1) – (3).

In answering question (3), I defended a descriptive theory of reference. Descriptive theories rely essentially on the notion of the intentional states of users of a language. Quine's doctrine of the indeterminacy of translation of sentences implies that there is no fact of the matter about imputations of intentions such as beliefs, so if he is right we must adopt a non-realist attitude towards them. Before question (3) could be answered it was therefore necessary to consider what arguments he has to support his doctrine. Moreover, if a realist proposes a descriptive theory of reference then it is incumbent upon him to explain how evidence is to be obtained about the intentions of language users. Chapter 3 thus served the double purpose of refuting a Quinean doctrine and grounding a subsequent theory.

Unlike the approach taken in Chapter 2, in Chapter 3 I went beyond Quine's strictures in two different but related respects. The first was in supporting the approach of Davidson, which broadens the scope of the enquiry from translation of language to interpretation of behaviour. I supplemented this in various ways. I drew on my refutation of the doctrine of the inscrutability of reference to explain why there need be nothing relative about the attribution of an alien ontology and I suggested that, particularly in the case of interpreting previous scientific theories, there would be considerably more evidence available for interpretation than might be supposed if Quine's description of radical translation were taken as the only model. The second respect in which I exceeded Quine's strictures was in explaining that both the radical translator and the radical interpreter could make use of non-behavioural facts in coming to understand an alien language. Indeed, Quine's own argument for indeterminacy assumes that the only facts relevant to translation are behavioural. But behavioural facts form only a small part of the totality of physical facts. One important class of non-behavioural fact is that indicating causal relations as, for example, between an experimenter and his subject-matter. Such relations are rightly emphasized by those who have argued for a causal, or non-descriptive, account of reference. For these reasons I concluded both that Quine had failed to show that translation is indeterminate, and that a realist could pursue a descriptive theory of reference.

It should be emphasized that I did not claim that sentence translation, or even interpretation, will always be determinate. The available evidence is what decides the matter. If we have an insufficient body of published writings, or if we are just too distant in space and time from those who held apparently different scientific theories, then we may well have to conclude that we cannot now decide precisely what they believed. We saw this in Chapter 5, particularly in connection with Gassendi's atomic theory and the chemistry of the later phlogiston theorists, and more generally with theories such as Newton's mechanics where it might well turn out that we cannot determine precisely how to translate every theoretical statement. But such isolated examples are quite different from the Quinean doctrines, for they show only that translation can be underdetermined by the available evidence, not that it is indeterminate.

I went on in Chapter 4 to defend a cluster theory of reference for proper names and natural kind predicates. This was contrasted with the position of Kripke and Putnam who supported an account based on causal relations. Such an account is, I suggested, relevant to the epistemological question, (2), of how we can discover what the extension is of a natural kind predicate. It throws no light on the conceptual question, (3), of what it is for a natural kind predicate to have an extension.

One of the important features of a cluster theory of reference is that it enables us to allow for error on the part of our ancestors. In order for us to conclude that, say, Newton's term 'mass' had the same extension as "rest mass" in relativity theory, it is not necessary that Newton possessed every belief we now have about rest mass; a suitable majority will suffice. Here again the very possibility of reaching such a conclusion relies on the evidence forthcoming when we try to interpret what has been left to us by earlier theorists. In this sense the output of the theory of reference is empirically constrained.

This point was taken up in Chapter 5 where I explained how the realist could implement the methodology described in Chapters 3 and 4. The three case studies I presented were each of a different kind. The first, concerning Dalton's use of the natural kind predicate "atom", was one where there seems to be good evidence for assigning it an extension according to the chemical theory which succeeded Dalton's. In such a case the realist's view of scientific progress is vindicated, for successive theories turned out to be about the same things. The second study concerned the predicate "phlogiston". In conformity with our theory of interpretation, we made a distinction between *our* ascribing an extension to a predicate used in a previous theory (and not by us) and the previous theorists *themselves* assigning an extension to it. In addition, I argued that "phlogiston" was not a simple predicate from our standpoint, and that in order to interpret the behaviour of phlogiston chemists we were required to specify its extension for them using a complex disjunctive predicate. Once this is done the example also supports the realist's view of scientific progress in the sense that it enables us, from our theoretical standpoint, to assign an extension to a predicate used by our ancestors. In addition it provided us with an explanation of why phlogiston theory was eventually abandoned. The final study was of the functor "mass" as it occurred in Newtonian physics. Following Putnam, I characterized "mass" as a law-cluster term, thus suggesting that the way it referred could be explained using a cluster theory of reference. Even when this is done, though, it seems that to see in relativity theory a successor to Newton's physics we may need to rely on an additional criterion of interpretation, in some ways similar to that arising from the causal account of reference, viz, that we should aim to preserve mathematical structure when interpreting successive theories.

What these case studies also show is that the truth of the realist's claim that competing or successive theories are usually about the same things is a contingent matter. It depends on the information we have available for interpretation. In a sense the realist is offering a *theory* of scientific progress, a theory which can be tested against the evidence. As I have tried to suggest, there are many instances which support this theory. But I have not tried to rule out other accounts. The main burden of my argument has been to refute those *a priori* doctrines which would prevent the realist's account from receiving a fair test – particularly the *in*scrutability of reference of terms and the *in*determinacy of translation of sentences – and to explain what it is that has to be tested. In some places my argument has been programmatic rather than detailed. I hope to have convinced the reader that the details really are worth pursuing. For the realist explanation of how science progresses is not just intuitively appealing; it has a sound basis in the philosophy of language.

Bibliography

Avogadro, A. 1811. Essay on a manner of determining the relative masses of the elementary molecules of bodies, and the proportions in which they enter into these compounds. Reprinted in *Foundations of the Molecular Theory*, Alembic Club Reprint, No. 4, 28–51.

Boorse, C. 1975. The origins of the indeterminacy thesis, *Journal of Philosophy* **72**, 369–87.

Cajori, F. 1962. *History of Physics*, New York.

Churchland, P. M. 1979. *Scientific Realism and the Plasticity of Mind*, Cambridge.

Dalton, J. 1808. *A New System of Chemical Philosophy*, Part 1, Manchester.

Davidson, D. 1973*a*. Radical interpretation, *Dialectica* **27**, 313–28.

1973*b*. In defence of Convention T. In *Truth, Syntax and Modality*, ed. H. Leblanc, 76–86, Amsterdam.

1973*c*. On the very idea of a conceptual scheme, *Proceedings and Addresses of the American Philosophical Association* **47**, 5–20.

1974. Belief and the basis of meaning, *Synthese* **27**, 309–23.

1975. Thought and talk. In *Mind and Language*, ed. S. Guttenplan, 7–23, Oxford.

Duhem, P. 1954. *The Aim and Structure of Physical Theory*, trans. P. Wiener, Princeton.

Dummett, M. 1958. Truth, *Aristotelian Society Proceedings* **59**, 141–62.

1973. *Frege, Philosophy of Language*, Duckworth.

1974. Postscript, *Synthese* **27**, 523–34.

1975. Wang's paradox, *Synthese* **30**, 301–24.

Earman, J. 1977. Against indeterminacy, *Journal of Philosophy* **74**, 535–538.

Earman, J. & Friedman, M. 1973. The meaning and status of Newton's law of inertia, *Philosophy of Science* **40**, 329–59.

Evans, G. 1973. The causal theory of names, *Aristotelian Society*, suppl. vol. 47, 187–208.

1975. Identity and predication, *Journal of Philosophy* **72**, 343–64.

Feyerabend, P. K. 1962. Explanation, reduction, and empiricism. In *Minnesota Studies in the Philosophy of Science*, Vol. 3, ed. H. Feigl & G. Maxwell, 28–97, Minneapolis.

1965. Problems of empiricism. In *Beyond the Edge of Certainty*, ed. R. Colodny, 145–260, New Jersey.

Field, H. 1973. Theory change and the indeterminacy of reference, *Journal of Philosophy* **70**, 462–81.

1974. Quine and the correspondence theory, *Philosophical Review*, **83**, 200–28.

Fine, K. 1975. Vagueness, truth and logic, *Synthese* **30**, 265–300.

Føllesdal, D. 1975. Meaning and experience. In *Mind and Language*, ed. S. Guttenplan, 25–44. Oxford.

Frege, G. 1892. Über Sinn und Bedeutung. English translation: On sense and reference. In *Translations from the Philosophical Writings of Gottlob Frege*, ed. M. Black & P. Geach, 2nd edn., 56–78, Oxford 1970.

Grandy, R. 1973. Reference, meaning, and belief, *Journal of Philosophy* **70**, 439–52.

Hacking, I. 1975. *Why Does Language Matter to Philosophy?*, Cambridge.

Hill, C. 1971. Gavagai, *Analysis* **32**, 68–75.

Hookway, C. 1978. Indeterminacy and interpretation. In *Action and Interpretation*, ed. C. Hookway & P. Pettit, 17–41, Cambridge.

Jardine, N. 1978. "Realistic" realism and the progress of science. In *Action and Interpretation*, ed. C. Hookway & P. Pettit, 107–25, Cambridge.

Kripke, S. A. 1972*a*. Naming and necessity. In *Semantics of Natural Language*, ed. D. Davidson & G. Harman, 253–355, Dordrecht.

1972*b*. Addenda. In *Semantics of Natural Language*, ed. D. Davidson & G. Harman, 763–9, Dordrecht.

Kuhn, T. 1970. *The Structure of Scientific Revolutions*, 2nd edn., Chicago.

Lewis, D. 1974. Radical interpretation, *Synthese* **27**, 331–44.

McGinn, C. 1977. Charity, interpretation and belief, *Journal of Philosophy* **74**, 521–35.

Mendel, G. 1865. Experiments in plant-hybridization. Reprinted in *Experiments in plant-hybridization*, ed. J. Bennett, Edinburgh 1965.

Nagel, E. 1961. *The Structure of Science*, London.

Newton-Smith, W. 1978. The underdetermination of theory by datum, *Aristotelian Society*, suppl. vol. 52, 71–91.

Putnam, H. 1962. The analytic and the synthetic. In *Minnesota Studies in the Philosophy of Science*, vol. 3, ed. H. Feigl & G. Maxwell, 358–97, Minneapolis. Reprinted in Putnam (1975*b*), 33–69. References are to the reprint.

1973. Explanation and reference. In *Conceptual Change*, ed. G. Pearce & P. Maxwell, 199–221, Dordrecht. Reprinted in Putnam (1975*b*), 196–214. References are to the reprint.

1974. Comment on Wilfrid Sellars, *Synthese* **27** , 445–55.

1975*a*. The meaning of "meaning". In *Minnesota Studies in the Philosophy of Science*, Vol. 7, ed. K. Gunderson, 131–93, Minneapolis. Reprinted in Putnam (1975*b*), 215–71. References are to the reprint.

1975*b*. *Mind, Language and Reality: Philosophical Papers, Volume 2*, Cambridge.

1978. *Meaning and the Moral Sciences*, London.

Quine, W. V. 1953. Two dogmas of empiricism. In *From a Logical Point of View*. Cambridge, Mass.

1960. *Word and Object*, Cambridge, Mass.

131

1969a. Ontological relativity. In his *Ontological Relativity and Other Essays*, 26–68, New York.

1969b. Existence and quantification. In his *Ontological Relativity and Other Essays*, 91–113, New York.

1969c. Reply to Chomsky. In *Words and Objections*, ed. D. Davidson & J. Hintikka, 302–11, Dordrecht.

1969d. Reply to Strawson. In *Words and Objections*, ed. D. Davidson & J. Hintikka, 320–5, Dordrecht.

1970. On the reasons for indeterminacy of translation, *Journal of Philosophy* **67**, 178–83.

1974. Comment on Donald Davidson, *Synthese* **27**, 325–9.

Rorty, R. 1976. Realism and reference, *Monist* **59**, 321–40.

1980. *Philosophy and the Mirror of Nature*, Oxford.

Scheffler, I. 1967. *Science and Subjectivity*, Indianapolis.

Searle, J. 1958. Proper names, *Mind* **67**, 166–73. Reprinted in *Philosophical Logic*, ed. P. Strawson, 89–96, Oxford 1967.

Sellars, W. 1968. *Science and Metaphysics: Variations on Kantian Themes*, London.

1973. Conceptual change. In *Conceptual Change*, ed. G. Pearce & P. Maynard, Amsterdam.

Shapere, D. 1966. Meaning and scientific change. In *Mind and Cosmos*, ed. R. Colodny, 41–85, Pittsburgh.

Strawson, P. F. 1954. *Individuals*, London.

1969. Singular terms and predication. In *Words and Objections*, ed. D. Davidson & J. Hintikka, 97–117, Dordrecht.

Swinburne, R. G. 1969. Vagueness, inexactness, and imprecision, *British Journal for the Philosophy of Science* **19**, 281–99.

Tarski, A. 1956. The concept of truth in formalized languages. Reprinted in *Logic, Semantics, Metamathematics*, Oxford.

Wittgenstein, L. 1953. *Philosophical Investigations*, Oxford.

Wright, C. 1975. On the coherence of vague predicates, *Synthese* **30**, 325–65.

Zadeh, L. A. 1975. Fuzzy logic and approximate reasoning, *Synthese* **30**, 407–28.

Zemach, E. 1976. Putnam's theory on the reference of substance terms, *Journal of Philosophy* **73**, 116–27.

Index

Abelard, Peter, 90
action, theory of, 27–8, 51
analytical hypotheses, 22, 24, 28, 48,
  50, 58
Archimedes, 77, 81, 88
Aristotle, 10, 34, 93
Avogadro, A., 10, 62, 70, 108–12, 118,
  122

benefit of the doubt, principle of,
  114–16
Bohr, N., 2, 13, 70, 93, 104, 105, 113,
  117
Boorse, C., 61n
Brahe, Tycho, 2

Cajori, F., 73
causal account of reference, 14, 15,
  65–6, 86–91, 106, 127
causal condition for determining
  reference: of a natural kind
  predicate, 65–6, 68, 93, 105–6, 110,
  112, 122; of a proper name, 90, 105
charity, principle of, 24, 27, 52–6, 58,
  62, 105, 110, 113–14, 117
Churchland, P. M., 73
cluster theory of reference, 14, 17,
  Ch4, 116, 127, 128
Convention T, 55, 56, 60; T-sentences,
  55–7, 59, 60, 61, 63, 74, 78, 105, 114;
  see also truth
Copernicus, N., 10
correspondence theory of truth, 1, 2,
  21
crucial experiments, 6–7

Dalton, J., 2, 10, 61–70, 93, 106–12,
  114, 118, 122, 126, 128
Davidson, D., 27, 29, 52–70, 83, 93,
  110, 126
descriptive theory of reference, 3,
  76–7, 126–7

Dewey, J., 68
division of linguistic labour, principle
  of, 75, 98
Dummett, M., 28, 72, 75, 81, 87–8, 92,
  94, 96–7, 101

Earman, J., 123–4
Einstein, Albert, 6, 121, 122
Erigena, 89
essentialism, 72, 84–5, 100–2
Evans, G., 27–33, 39, 43, 44, 87–9
extension of a predicate, 9–16, 46, 54,
  Ch. 4, 104–28

falsificationist explanation of scientific
  progress, 2, 4, 6–7, 125
Feyerabend, P., 5–8, 61, 119, 124
Field, H., 21, 78–9, 116, 122–4
Fine, K., 92
Føllesdal, D., 68
four questions for realism, see realism,
  four questions for
Franklin, B., 66, 68
Frege, G., 8, 9, 16, 25, 46, 74, 76, 84,
  92
Friedman, M., 123

Galileo, 4, 5
Gassendi, P., 117, 127
gavagai, 21–44, 48–9
Gay-Lussac, J., 62, 107–8
Gilbert and Sullivan, 79
Goodman, N., 43
Grandy, R., 28, 52

Hacking, I., 62
Harman, G., 25
Hill, C., 38–40
Hookway, C., 51, 52
humanity, principle of, 28
Huyghens, C., 6

133

identity, in translation, 22–3, 33, 39–42, 59
incommensurability, 7, 8, 11, 12, 21, 119, 125
indeterminacy of translation of sentences, 16–18, 27–8, Ch. 3, 70, 106, 110, 124, 126, 129; relation to inscrutability of reference of terms, 18–21, 69, 124, 126
indexical predicates, 99–102
inscrutability of reference of terms, 16–17, Ch. 2, 58–9, 62, 67, 106, 110, 124, 126, 129; relation to indeterminancy of translation of sentences, 18–21, 69, 124, 126
interpretation, theory of, 17, 27, Ch. 3, 70, 104, 109–10, 126; prerequisite for theory of reference, 70, 78, 109–10, 126; see also radical interpretation

Jardine, N., 113–17
Johannsen, W., 104
John the Scot, 89

Kepler, J., 2, 4
Kripke, S., 54., 65, 72, 80–91, 95–8, 100–3, 127
Kuhn, T., 7, 117n

Lavoisier, A., 118
law-cluster terms, 120–2, 128
Lewis, D., 27, 28, 52
linguistic community, 12, 14, 46–7, 52, 55–6, 73–4, 94, 99, 115
logical derivability, condition of, 5, 119
Lombard, Peter, 90

McGinn, C., 53–4, 83
mass, 5–6, 8, 78–9, 119–24, 128
mathematical structure, as a criterion in interpretation, 123–4, 128
Maxwell, J. C., 93
meaning, 7–9, 13, 47, 48, 51–2, 61, 63, 67–9, 80, 105, 110, 119, 125; invariance, condition of, 5, 119–20; of a predicate, 94, 98–103; of a proper name, 74–90; theory of, 29–33; see also sense
mechanics: Galilean, 4, 5; Newtonian, 4–6, 78–9, 119–24; special relativity, 5–6, 78–9, 119–24
Mendel, G., 10, 65, 68, 114, 121

Mendeleyev, D., 93
Michelson and Morley, 6
Muller, H., 13, 70, 93, 113, 121

Nagel, E., 5, 119
natural kind predicates, 10–11, 19, 46, 54, 66, Ch. 4, 120
network model of theories/language, 60–1; see also observational sentences
Newton, I., 2, 4, 5, 78–9, 107, 114, 121–4, 127–8

observational, relation to theoretical, 6, 61, 62, 64, 110
observational sentences, 49, 57, 59, 60–4, 67, 105, 110; see also theoretical sentences
observational terms, 6, 47, 61, 71; see also theoretical terms
ontological relativity, 21, 57, 58

partial denotation, 21, 78–9, 116
phlogiston, 13, 14, 71, 112–18, 127–8
physical magnitude terms, 65–6, 72–3
Popper, K., 6
positivist explanation of scientific progress, 2, 4–7, 119, 125
possible worlds, 85–6
predication, problem of, 1, 21
proper names, theory of reference for, 74–91
Ptolemy, 10, 13, 93, 113, 121, 122
Putnam, H, 13, 14, 65–66, 68, 71–2, 75, 81, 94–5, 98–103, 120–1, 127, 128

quantification: recognition of, in translation, 38–9; referential, 38–9; substitutional, 38–9, 58
Quine, W. V., 16, 17, Ch. 2, Ch. 3, 70, 110, 126–7

radical interpretation, 51–69, 126–7; see also interpretation, theory of; radical translation
radical translation, 21–4, 46–58, 62, 126–7; see also indeterminacy of translation of sentences; radical interpretation
realism, four questions for, 10–17, Conclusion; question (1), 11–12, 15, 17, Ch. 5, 125; question (2), 12–17, 80, 90, 92–3, 104–6, 109,

Conclusion; question (3), 14–17, 46, 70–103, 109, 116, Conclusion; question (4), 16–17, 18–45, Conclusion
realist explanation of scientific progress, 2, 7–17, 70, 118, 119, 125, 128; contingent truth of, 3, 70–1, 106, 112, 117, 128–9
reference, 3, 9, 16, 46, 74; problem of, 1, 21; theory of, dependent of a theory of interpretation, 70, 78, 109–110, 126; theory of, necessary for explanation of scientific progress, 3, 8n, 117–18, 125; *see also* causal account of reference; causal condition for determining reference; inscrutability of reference of terms; proper names, theory of reference for
relativism, 2, 7, 125
rigid designators, 100
Rorty, R., 117–18
Rutherford, E., 70

Scheffler, I., 8n
scientific progress, problem of 1, 1–2, 125; falsificationist explanation of, 2, 4, 6–7, 125; positivist explanation of, 2, 4–7, 119, 125; realist explanation of, 2, 7–17, 70, 118, 119, 125, 128
Searle, J., 77
sense, 9, 13–14, 46, 94; as distinct from meaning, 9, 94–5; of a name, 74–6, 79–81, 83–5; of a predicate, 13–14, 16, 94; *see also* meaning
Shapere, D., 8
singular terms, 9; translation of, 34–8, 43, 44

Stoney, G. J., 73, 102, 104
Strawson, P. F., 36, 77
Swinburne, R. G., 92

Tarski, A., 11, 52, 55, 58
Taylor, I., 87
theoretical, relation to observational, 6, 61, 62, 64, 110;
theoretical sentences, 57, 60, 67; *see also* observational sentences
theoretical terms, 6, 47, 61, 71; *see also* observational terms
translation, between theories, 8, 16, 106; *see also* indeterminacy of translation of sentences; radical translation
truth: correspondence theory of, 1, 2, 21; Tarski's definition of, 52, 55–6, 58; theory of, 53, 55, 56, 58, 60, 61, 63, 69, 78, 110; *see also* Convention T.
truth-value gaps, 36

underdetermination of theory by evidence, 18, 47–51, 59–60, 64, 67–9, 117, 124, 127

vague predicates, 91–2

Wilson, N. L., 27
Wittgenstein, L., 76–7
Wright, C., 92

Young, T., 6

Zadeh, L. A., 92
Zemach, E., 72, 99, 101

For EU product safety concerns, contact us at Calle de José Abascal, 56–1°,
28003 Madrid, Spain or eugpsr@cambridge.org.

www.ingramcontent.com/pod-product-compliance
Ingram Content Group UK Ltd.
Pitfield, Milton Keynes, MK11 3LW, UK
UKHW012339130625
459647UK00009B/387